DESIGN FOR SIX SIGMA

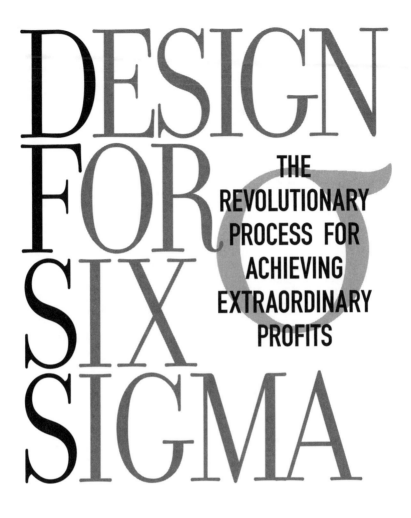

DESIGN FOR SIX SIGMA

THE REVOLUTIONARY PROCESS FOR ACHIEVING EXTRAORDINARY PROFITS

SUBIR CHOWDHURY

Dearborn™
Trade Publishing
A **Kaplan Professional** Company

This publication is designed to provide accurate and authoritative information in regard to the subject matter covered. It is sold with the understanding that the publisher is not engaged in rendering legal, accounting, or other professional service. If legal advice or other expert assistance is required, the services of a competent professional person should be sought.

Senior Acquisitions Editor: Jean Iversen
Senior Managing Editor: Jack Kiburz
Interior Design: Lucy Jenkins
Cover Design: Scott Rattray, Rattray Design
Typesetting: the dotted i

Published by Dearborn Trade Publishing, a Kaplan Professional Company

Printed in the United States of America

02   03   04   10   9   8   7   6   5   4   3   2   1

Library of Congress Cataloging-in-Publication Data

Chowdhury, Subir.
    Design for Six Sigma : the revolutionary process for achieving extraordinary profits / Subir Chowdhury.
        p.   cm.
    Includes bibliographical references and index.
    ISBN 0-7931-5224-0 (6x9 hardcover)
    1. Quality control—Statistical methods.   2. Experimental design.
I. Title.
TS156 .C532 2002
658.5′62—dc21

2002000193

Dearborn Trade books are available at special quantity discounts to use for sales promotions, employee premiums, or educational purposes. Please call our Special Sales Department to order or for more information, at 800-621-9621, ext. 4410, or write Dearborn Trade Publishing, 155 N. Wacker Drive, Chicago, IL 60606-1719.

ADVANCE PRAISE

"In his latest book, *Design for Six Sigma*, Chowdhury effectively communicates how to turn Six Sigma strategy into breakthrough performance. Chowdhury's excellent contribution shows how to make Six Sigma part of the way we work—the unifying framework to align and energize an entire company."

—Dave B. Burritt, Six Sigma Deployment Champion, Caterpillar Inc.

"Subir Chowdhury has written the quintessential book on Design for Six Sigma that fills a critical need for published material on the subject. This innovative book provides a clear road map for all executives, business managers, and Six Sigma leaders who are engaged in the competitive race to build cost-effective, defect-free processes and products that will win customers and guarantee their loyalty."

—Cynthia Callas, Vice President of Six Sigma Deployment/Black Belt, Merrill Lynch

"Why design a process that isn't optimal and will only need Six Sigma improvements later? Subir Chowdhury's most important and timely book lays the groundwork using DFSS tools to design the process correctly the first time, thus saving time, effort, money, and most of all customer frustration."

—Richard (Dick) Cunningham, Executive Six Sigma Champion and Director of Operational
& Business Excellence, Johns Manville Corporation—*a Berkshire Hathaway Company*

"Written in an easy-to-read story format, Chowdhury's previous book, *The Power of Six Sigma*, provides a clear understanding of how Six Sigma can benefit any business activity. I award all Project Champions a copy as they complete their training workshop and recommend all others read it as well. Chowdhury's *Design for Six Sigma* promises to be just as powerful and helpful."

—Douglas R. Pratt, P.E., Director, Six Sigma Process Excellence, Dow Corning Corporation

"In order to truly attain Six Sigma status, following the process outlined in Chowdhury's book, *Design for Six Sigma* (DFSS), is crucial. DFSS will help your company greatly increase its competitive strength."

—Rob Lindner, Vice President, Corporate Quality, Sunbeam Corporation

"Whether your product is the result of a complex technical manufacturing process or group-driven ideation, *Design for Six Sigma* offers a framework to get it right the first time. With this important and outstanding new book, Subir Chowdhury drives home the need for today's businesses to understand their customers before trying to service them."

—Roxanne O'Brasky, President, International Society of Six Sigma Professionals (ISSSP)

This book would never have materialized without the continuous help of the following colleagues and friends:

ALAN WU
BARRY BEBB
SHIN TAGUCHI
BRAD WALKER

ASI–American Supplier Institute

DEDICATION

To my friend, coauthor, and mentor **Dr. Genichi Taguchi.**

CONTENTS

 **PREFACE**

Virtually every American over the age of 25 recalls the day in early 1986 when the space shuttle Challenger exploded just 73 seconds after lifting off from Cape Canaveral's launchpad. All aboard died, including America's darling, Christa McAuliffe, who was chosen from 11,000 other American teachers to become the first teacher in space.

Like so many tragedies, part of the horror of the Challenger disaster is how easily it could have been avoided. As the *Guardian* reported: "Roger Boisjoly, a senior engineer at Morton-Thiokol— the contractors that built the solid rocket boosters for the space shuttle—had been airing doubts about the Challenger's O-rings for at least six months before the disaster. A year earlier he'd gone to Florida to inspect the spent rockets from a previous mission. He had been amazed at the condition of the joints. The primary seal had failed and allowed hot gas to surge by."

In addition to the terrible loss of life, the Challenger disaster also cost the United States billions of dollars and set back NASA's cause several years—all because of a cheap, simple part that NASA had already been warned was faulty. Likewise, the Concorde crash of July 2000 not only killed all 113 people on board, it prompted an investigation that grounded all Concorde flights for months, costing more than $30 million to ensure that the remaining fleet was safe.

And in the United States, Bridgestone/Firestone will pay up to $51.5 million to settle claims over allegedly faulty tires that have been linked to 271 deaths and more than 800 injuries. The reputation of the Ford Explorer has suffered in the process, too. Ford, the world's number-two automaker, and Firestone ended their nearly 100-year-old relationship in a dispute over who is to blame.

Such tragedies make us rethink the way we live and work. On the one hand, we're reminded of how fragile life is and of how easily things can go wrong at any moment. But on the other hand, smart businesspeople are reminded of the importance of quality in everything they do, and how such events can be avoided if they keep their focus on doing their best work at every turn.

When I meet with CEOs or senior executives across the globe, I find that very few truly practice *prevention* as a strategy. I think the reason is simple: Putting out fires is glamorous, preventing them is not. In most companies, those who quell potential disasters get all the glory, but the quiet workers who ensure that those disasters never occur in the first place don't get half the attention or rewards. In the 21st century, customers have come to demand perfection in their products and services, and if you can't deliver, they'll go elsewhere.

The irony is that most senior executives understand the importance of quality—it's been beaten into them for decades—and truly believe they know the secrets of how to achieve perfection in their line of work. It's the same Ford Motor Company, after all, that embraced Dr. W. Edwards Deming's legendary philosophy of quality in the 1980s. Two decades later, in 2001, Ford's chief operating officer Nick Scheele said: "When I say we need to get back to basics, what I mean is we emphasize our products and our quality."

It's been my experience that most executives harbor misconceptions about the many quality initiatives that have bombarded U.S. companies over the past two decades. This book will clarify these misconceptions. The first, and most important, misconception to dispel is that Design for Six Sigma (DFSS) only applies to engineering designs. Given the name Design for Six Sigma, this confusion is understandable but costly if not corrected, because DFSS can be applied with equal effectiveness to such varied tasks as billing, marketing, customer service, and everything in between. DFSS will also teach you how to determine what your customers truly want and optimize your operations at every turn to give it to them.

I wrote this book with the belief that designing products and processes right the first time MUST be every company's first concern. The most visionary CEOs lead their teams with this focus in mind. This book is not just for CEOs, but also for those engineering managers who believe they know what Robust Design® is all about and end up fighting fire after fire when a product is actually launched. And it's for those operations managers who call consulting firms to fix their own processes. Finally, this book is for anyone who wants to serve customers effectively and efficiently by understanding the true customer's voice.

When I asked my very good friend, the late Philip B. Crosby, to give me his take on Six Sigma a few years ago, he answered with a question: "Which is better—3.4 defects per million opportunities or zero?" That's the difference between Six Sigma—an incredibly high rate of perfection—and perfection itself. That was Phil's attitude.

The same year, when I put the same question to another close colleague of mine, Dr. Genichi Taguchi, his response was: "Why not Seven Sigma?" Both Crosby and Taguchi stressed thinking about quality "upstream" instead of "downstream"— in other words, where the process *begins,* not where it ends. That's what Design for Six Sigma is all about—focusing on preventions instead of cures.

As I mentioned in my previous book, *The Power of Six Sigma,* although Six Sigma and Design for Six Sigma are fundamentally different quality initiatives, they both rely on combining *People Power* with *Process Power.* At a recent Harvard Business School gathering, former GE Chairman and CEO (and Six Sigma devotee) Jack Welch said: "You have to be sure every day that you're turning people on." Focusing on the people doing the work—

and not just abstract theories—is the key ingredient to make any change last in your company. Design for Six Sigma is uniquely qualified to inspire, guide, and motivate your employees and colleagues to do their best work for the team.

I openly confess that it really does not matter who is preaching the virtues of Six Sigma or Design for Six Sigma, because the tools used in both of these powerful management strategies are nothing new. They have been around for decades. But how successful your organization is depends entirely on how effectively those tools are applied. Several organizations have already deployed Design for Six Sigma after their initial Six Sigma success but will likely fail on their DFSS initiatives, because they are misapplying the DFSS methodology and tools.

Six Sigma's trademark methodology of DMAIC (Define, Measure, Analyze, Improve, and Control) has become a standard operating procedure in companies around the globe. Unfortunately, in DFSS there is little consistency among practitioners about the terms that define the process. As a result, the acronyms range from DMADV to DMEDI to IDDOV. The good news is that it really does not matter what you call it. The DFSS methodology is still a straightforward, five-step process, just as is Six Sigma's DMAIC.

Most consulting firms require fewer training days to teach Black Belts (the program's movers and shakers) about DFSS than they do for Six Sigma (about 5 to 10 days compared to 16 to 20 days). However, everyone involved rightly stresses that DFSS is more rigorous to implement than Six Sigma, in part because the practitioners must master more quality concepts such as Quality Function Deployment and Robust Design. This book will clear out all the cobwebs and let you and your people get right to work on exciting projects that bring results.

At this writing, *Design for Six Sigma* is the first book on DFSS. With so many business writers and consultants out there these days, I'm a little surprised that I am the first. Not only have countless businesspeople been clamoring for a book on DFSS, but in my discussions with business executives and managers, they have repeatedly asked for a quick read that is not overly technical and is reader friendly. I have done my best to honor this request with this book. The book in your hands is not a technical how-to book but an easy-to-understand explanation of Design for Six Sigma that will help you and your company in dramatic fashion.

The book opens with an introductory chapter on Design for Six Sigma and also reviews the basics of its predecessor, Six Sigma, and explains the differences between the two. Chapters 2 and 3 explain the roles employees fulfill in DFSS Projects and how they're implemented, while Chapters 4 through 7 take the reader on a detailed tour of each phase of the five-step process (Identify, Define, Develop, Optimize, and Verify, or IDDOV) of the DFSS management strategy. My goal is to answer virtually all the questions anyone new to DFSS may have.

I will consider this book a success if I can help business-people and organizations deploy DFSS effectively. It would bring me a deep sense of satisfaction if, because of such companies' renewed emphasis on quality through DFSS, we all see fewer innocent victims of corporate carelessness, such as those that resulted in the tragedies mentioned above.

Someday, we'll all lead our organizations the DFSS way!

Subir Chowdhury
Executive Vice President, ASI–American Supplier Institute
E-mail: subir.chowdhury@asiusa.com
Web site: <www.asiusa.com>

CHAPTER 1

DFSS: The ONLY Way to Achieve Six Sigma

Business theories come and go, as everyone knows, but a new concept called Six Sigma has planted roots deep enough in the pantheon of Fortune 500 companies to stand the test of time.

General Electric, Allied Signal, Caterpillar, DuPont, Sears, American Express, Merrill Lynch, Dow Chemical, United Technologies, Raytheon, and Ford Motor Company, among many others, have already devoted a half-dozen years, well over a billion dollars, and hundreds of thousands of employees to the effort. And it's paying off by dramatically cutting costs, reducing mistakes, boosting worker morale, and bolstering the companies' profits. Through Six Sigma, GE, for example, cranked up its 2000 earnings per share $1.27, up 19 percent; 2000 revenues grew 16 percent to $130 billion; and earnings rose 19 percent to $12.7 billion.

But as I freely confessed on the final page of my previous book, *The Power of Six Sigma*, implementing Six Sigma can only take a company so far. The organizations that want to reach the next level of efficiency need to adopt a program called Design for Six Sigma (DFSS). Where Six Sigma focuses on streamlining the production and business process to eliminate mistakes, improve morale, and save money, Design for Six Sigma starts earlier, to develop or redesign the process itself, so fewer wrinkles show up in the first place, thus systematically preventing downstream errors.

It's the difference between getting a tune-up and a brand-new engine; between patching your pants and getting a new pair. Instead of constantly debugging products and processes that already exist—an effort that never ends, of course—DFSS starts from scratch to design the product or process to be virtually error free. This effectively replaces the usual trial-and-error style with a cleaner, bump-free end-result that also requires much less aftermarket tinkering. It's the classic "pay me now or pay me later" solution, in which more time and effort are spent upfront so less will be spent after the fact.

Smart carpenters say, "Measure twice and cut once." And that's what Design for Six Sigma is about: getting it right the first time. If the design or process was flawed in the first place, you can only go so far with downstream fixes. In the case of producing products, manufacturing can only *take quality away* from the design, not improve it, so we must do our best to make the design as flawless as possible before we implement it.

NOT JUST FOR ENGINEERS

I strongly believe that design is not the private domain of engineers. Design is everyone's business. Our jobs may or may not be designed for us, but we design how we perform them. We design projects. We design processes. We design presentations, reports, and plans. Design for Six Sigma can be effectively and successfully applied to virtually every activity we perform every day.

Examples include designing a more cost-effective, error-free overnight delivery system; designing a lighter-weight, more durable hubcap that doesn't bend or break when the tire hits a pothole; designing a more streamlined internal mail system for your company that reduces lost and misdirected interoffice correspondence; or designing cleaner, more pleasing presentation software that's easier to use. The point is: Designing isn't just for engineers anymore.

Design for Six Sigma has already proven to be a groundbreaking strategic initiative for the corporations that have thoroughly implemented the methodology, and it's no exaggeration to say it has the potential to become the most significant management initiative of the 21st century. While such bold statements are often used to promote the latest hot idea, there are times, of course, when they are actually true. From the early returns of DFSS companies, it already appears that this could be one of those times.

A RENEWED CALL FOR INNOVATION

Design for Six Sigma was created to enhance the one factor almost every CEO has identified as the single sustainable competitive advantage: innovation. The problem is, it's also one of the most difficult things to manage. While all employees must adhere to certain guidelines to work for any corporation, creativity must be given a wide berth to flourish. DFSS shows managers how to generate more creativity from their staffs in a way that will not only preserve the integrity of the company, it will actually strengthen the company through better ideas, happier employees, and an environment that encourages growth instead of stifling it.

Design for Six Sigma provides the means to accelerate innovation, which is why GE, Caterpillar, Delphi Automotive Systems, Dow Chemical, and others have already entered the Design for Six Sigma race. Many others will follow just as they have in pursuing Six Sigma. Those who excel in Design for Six Sigma will win; those who don't will face a very perilous future.

A BRIEF REVIEW OF SIX SIGMA

Although this book is intended for executives and managers who already have a firm grasp of Six Sigma, please forgive me for giving a little rudimentary review to make sure we all have a fundamental understanding of Six Sigma before proceeding to the more advanced ideas in this book. To gain a better understanding of DFSS, therefore, a nickel tour of Six Sigma is in order.

In a nutshell, Six Sigma is a management philosophy focused on eliminating mistakes, waste, and rework. Where most programs focus on "offense"—that is, making more products, increasing volume, developing whiz-bang marketing concepts— Six Sigma focuses on "defense"—doing many of the things you're already doing, but doing them better, with fewer mistakes.

Therefore, instead of relying on more "run production" with more hits and home runs and stolen bases, Six Sigma takes the other, less common approach of concentrating on better fielding, better throwing, and better pitching. It might not be as glamorous as hitting more home runs, but virtually every season the World Series champion has the best pitching and fielding, too. Defense works.

It's important to point out here that, like DFSS, Six Sigma is not a rah-rah, "Do Better" program. It is not a motivational trick that simply bumps up employee efforts for a month or two. Instead, it establishes a measurable status to strive for, and embodies a strategic problem-solving method to increase customer satisfaction and dramatically enhance the bottom line. It teaches your employees how to improve the way they do business, scientifically and fundamentally, and maintain their new performance level for years to come.

Let's take a step back for a moment to define a few terms. *Sigma* is a Greek letter used to designate standard deviation, which is a measure of variation within a process. Golfers, for example, know that they will rarely get the same score twice. In five rounds of golf, for instance, one golfer might shoot 75, 78,

80, 82, and 85. Although he averages 80 per round, his range is plus or minus five strokes. His standard deviation would be less than that, but you've got the idea. Standard deviation measures how far he tends to stray from his average of 80.

In Six Sigma, standard deviation measures two things: how much one thing varies from a specific point or target—as with the golfer and his average of 80 strokes—and how much one thing varies from another. In golf, that would be the average difference between one golfer and another. In business terms it measures the capability of any given process to perform defect-free work. The higher the sigma value, the fewer defects you have—six being virtually perfect.

Example: Let's say you have a thermostat and you're trying to keep your room temperature at 70 degrees. The thermostat is supposed to perform within 67 to 73 degrees—which we will refer to as the "requirements" for the system. But this particular thermostat's fluctuation is only between 68 and 72. That's a pretty small amount of variation, so in this case, the process capability of the thermostat is acceptable. It's within the required range. But when the temperature is bouncing back and forth between 55 and 85 degrees, the spread would be a greater amount of variation and would not meet the requirements. This means the capability of the thermostat is unacceptable and must be adjusted.

Sigma—or standard deviation—is used to quantify how good or bad a process is performing by determining how far from the ideal it is functioning. In other words, how many mistakes a company makes, doing whatever it does, from manufacturing steel to delivering the morning paper.

HOW GOOD IS GOOD ENOUGH?

Six is the Sigma level of perfection we're shooting for. If your company's working at One Sigma, for example, that means it's making about 700,000 defects per million opportunities, or

DPMO. At One Sigma you're only doing things right about 30 percent of the time—a clearly unacceptable level of performance for everyone who doesn't play left field for the Yankees. Baseball is probably the only profession where a 30 percent success rate is considered very good.

Two Sigma is, obviously, better. If you're working at Two Sigma, you're making a little over 300,000 mistakes per million opportunities. In other words, you're batting about 70 percent. Great for a major leaguer, but just okay in business. Most companies operate between Three and Four Sigma, which means they make between approximately 67,000 and 6,000 mistakes per million opportunities. If you're operating at 3.8 Sigma, that means you're getting it right 99 percent of the time.

To most people, that sounds like virtual perfection—when actually, a 99-percent success rate is the equivalent of 20,000 lost articles of mail every hour, or 5,000 botched surgical procedures every week, or four accidents per day at major airports—levels of failure the American public would never accept, and rightly so. The whole point of the Six Sigma management philosophy is that 99 percent is not good enough. The goal of the Six Sigma process is just that, Six Sigma, which means making only 3.4 mistakes per million opportunities—in other words, getting it right 99.99966 percent of the time.

While this goal might seem impossible, there are actually companies out there who are consistently achieving between Five and Six Sigma quality. We'll discuss this more a little later, but the important point here is that they're not knocking themselves out to improve quality just for the sake of it. They're doing it to make more money by cutting costs and increasing profits.

Most companies think improving quality costs money, so they see the quality-versus-profits balance as a trade-off, a tug-of-war between their customers and their accountants. They ask themselves, how much quality can we afford to give the customers and still make a profit? But Six Sigma companies flip that around. They've learned that quality SAVES money, because you have fewer throw-outs, fewer warranty payouts, fewer refunds, and much higher rates of customer retention. And doing all that, in turn, increases profits.

It is amazing to me how much money companies spend to attract customers, and how little they do to keep them after they've got them. You only have so much influence on a customer who's never been to your store, so you've got to make sure you retain the person who is already in your store. To keep her as a loyal customer really isn't that hard, when you look at it a certain way. All you have to do is do exactly what you said you would in your advertisements: give her a good product and good service at a good price. Keep such customers and you don't need to advertise nearly as much. Customer satisfaction and retention is to marketing what good fielding is to good hitting. It's not as glamorous, as I've said, but it's at least as effective—and will give you a great advantage over your competitors who typically ignore it.

Now that you've had a refresher course on the definition of Six Sigma, let's explore how it works. The power of Six Sigma is the combination of People Power with Process Power. The bulk of the work on People Power is done by middle management. A company's most outstanding people with proven drive and intellect are chosen to become Black Belts, a Six Sigma term denoting those who are most responsible for running Six Sigma projects. They are trained extensively in the Six Sigma philosophy and tools, then given the support and resources they need to work full time on a specific project. Once the deadlines have been met and numerical goals have been reached, a Black Belt moves on to other projects.

Process Power, on the other hand, encompasses five steps: Define the problem, Measure where you stand, Analyze where the problem starts, Improve the situation, and Control the new process to confirm that it's fixed. That boils down to a simple acronym, DMAIC, or as some people have learned to memorize it: Dumb Managers Always Ignore Customers.

Some corporations that have adopted this process have thrived, including GE and AlliedSignal. But others may be implementing it ineffectively because they either miss the point of it themselves or can't communicate it effectively and accurately to their people. The first step, therefore, is understanding what Six Sigma is and how it works.

The second key to the success of Six Sigma is acceptance. This requires everyone in a company—from the CEOs to the factory workers—to understand and appreciate the true power and benefits of Six Sigma, so they'll buy into it 100 percent.

Despite the large number of incredible triumphs corporations have achieved in implementing Six Sigma, there seems to be a "Five Sigma Wall" that even the best companies run into—sort of like the "runner's wall" marathoners hit after about 20 miles into the race. In business, you can only get so far by picking the low hanging fruit—that is, designing the easiest projects to correct the easiest problems. Sooner or later you have to go for the tough stuff. So how do we do this?

The next challenge is to advance from a Five Sigma to a Six Sigma level of performance—and the only way to get there is through Design for Six Sigma, or DFSS.

WHAT IS DESIGN FOR SIX SIGMA?

The idea behind Six Sigma is simple: Instead of simply plugging leak after leak, the idea is to figure out WHY it's leaking and WHERE, and attack the problem at its source. But Six Sigma does not address the original design of the product or process, it merely improves them.

Design for Six Sigma is not simply a rehash of the lessons learned in Six Sigma, but a fundamentally different methodology. DFSS complements the Six Sigma improvement methodology, but takes it one step further—or really, one step back—ferreting out the flaws of the product and the process during the *design* stage—*not* the quality control stage, or even the production stage. While Six Sigma focuses on improving existing designs, DFSS concentrates its efforts on creating new and better ones.

If your company were a house, it would work like this: while most business initiatives focus only on plugging leaky pipes and fixtures, a Six Sigma approach would examine the process and discover that the quality of the welding and sink faucets was inadequate, and replace them. DFSS would take one step further back in the process by designing the system—before it was ever installed—with welds and fixtures it knew would produce Six Sigma quality, without repairs or redesigns.

Of course, few businesses involve leaky pipes. But all businesses involve customers—and understanding and pleasing them is the key, naturally, to business success.

Traditionally, most companies have not taken the time or made the effort that is required to learn what their customers really want. DFSS requires applying resources to finding out what customers really want, and then devoting the entire project to meeting the needs and desires of these customers. This works whether the customer is external—a car buyer, for example—or internal, such as the people in the accounting department.

BEGIN WITH THE END IN MIND

Most companies spend only 5 percent of their budget on design, but design typically accounts for 70 percent of the cost of the product—partly because 80 percent of quality problems are unwittingly *designed into* the product itself. In government contracts, 30 to 40 percent of the budget is set aside for testing and correcting the product—after-the-fact measures. Imagine! In advance, they're admitting that one-third of the budget must be devoted to correcting the problems they plan to create with the first two-thirds of the budget! If test and rework are planned for up front, it is a virtual certainty that test and rework will be performed. Plan for failure, and you'll get it.

DFSS rejects all this old-school thinking. The DFSS approach leads to clean designs that dramatically reduce the need for later inspection, test, and rework.

One reason the old way is so slow and expensive is due to something carpenters call "accrued error," which occurs when you make a slightly faulty measurement while you're building the foundation, after which that mistake gets magnified every time you build on top of it. By the time you're working on the roof, everything is so out of kilter you're forced to scrap your original plans and find a way to make it fit any way you can. Such expedience may get the job done but will result in untold problems down the road when the jury-rigged work has to be repaired or replaced.

In companies that don't follow DFSS, the "firefighters" who correct these endless errors as they crop up are the heroes of the organization, when the real heroes should be the people who design "fireproof" processes in the first place. Although fire prevention is not dramatic, it is a lot cheaper, a lot easier, and a lot more efficient than fire fighting.

A crucial aspect of DFSS is its pan-company approach. Instead of each department working independently, with its own agendas and bottom lines, DFSS calls for representatives from each division to sit down together in the *planning* stage to figure out how to reduce the number of steps necessary to get the job done. It's as if the masons, the rough carpenters, the drywallers, the electricians, and the plumbers got together to think it all through before anyone even picks up a hammer. This will cut costs and make the process easier for everyone up and down the line. Fewer steps, fewer mistakes, fewer fires to put out.

DFSS companies spend more time and money on the design phase than the traditional 5 percent that most companies spend. By spending more up front, they can dramatically shrink the 70 percent production costs of the finished products or services they create.

The goal is to replace as many inspectors as possible and put producers in their place. After all, it's the producers who produce the product—and make the money—creating a cost-effective trade-off. You get fewer changes in your original plans downstream, avoiding the countless ad hoc decisions so many companies are forced to make. You also spend less on resources, because there's less waste, and you get the intangible benefit of having all your employees committed to the entire project, not just their piece of the pie.

The best part for you, however, is that DFSS has already been tried and proven to work as advertised. Motorola applied DFSS to the design and production of one of its recent pagers, and according to *Consumer Reports*, it's virtually defect-proof. General Electric enrolled 20,000 of its employees in the DFSS program, so they could perfect everything from engine blades to responding to phone calls about service. And it has worked like a charm.

GE's annual reports from 1998, 1999, and 2000 tell a very compelling story when read in sequence, starting with the 1998 report:

> Every new GE product and service in the future will be DFSS—Designed for Six Sigma. These new offerings will truly take us to a new definition of "World Class."
>
> The first major products Designed for Six Sigma hit the marketplace and drew unprecedented customer accolades.
>
> They were, in essence, designed by the customer, using all of the critical-to-quality performance features (CTQs) the customer wanted in the product and then subjecting these CTQs to the rigorous statistical Design for Six Sigma process.

General Electric's 1999 annual report had this to say:

GE Medical Systems delivered record financial results in 1999, with revenue and earnings growth exceeding 25%. We introduced seven products in 1999 using Design for Six Sigma (DFSS) with more than 20 to be released in 2000. These products are different—they capture customer needs better and can be brought to market faster than ever before. We will sell more than two billion dollars worth of DFSS products by the end of 2000. (Jeffrey R. Immelt)

And from GE's 2000 annual report:

GE Medical Systems also introduced 22 Designed for Six Sigma (DFSS) products in 2000. Most significant among them were the Senographe® and Innov™ a proprietary digital X-ray systems that will revolutionize breast cancer detection and interventional cardiac imaging. In total, more than 50% of our sales will come from DFSS products in 2001. (Joseph M. Hogan)

Remember, Design for Six Sigma's effectiveness spans far beyond redesigning engineered products. Design for Six Sigma can be applied to internal business transactions, customer services, and just about anything that can benefit from innovative, streamlined, customer-friendly designs—which is, of course, almost everything.

Many business leaders view DFSS as the obvious sequel to Six Sigma, the second leg of this business biathlon they know they need to complete for their companies to reach their full potential. DFSS is already shaping up to be just as popular as Six Sigma. Anywhere Six Sigma goes, Design for Six Sigma is sure to follow—and in some cases, Design for Six Sigma should actually come first, despite what the Six Sigma promoters would have you believe. Six Sigma is not a prerequisite for Design for Six Sigma. In fact, Design for Six Sigma is not even dependent on Six Sigma.

WHY DESIGN FOR SIX SIGMA?

You might as well ask why football players need to know how to pass the ball when they already know how to run with it. Even devoted Six Sigma companies typically run into the wall as they approach Five Sigma, and can't figure out what to do to get to Six Sigma.

Visionary Fortune 500 CEOs understand this and are embracing DFSS accordingly. All the major Champions of Six Sigma—including GE, AlliedSignal, and Caterpillar—are investing at least as much time, personnel, and money into Design for Six Sigma as they did for Six Sigma.

While Six Sigma helps fix what is broken—which is obviously a needed tool for any company that's already up and running—Design for Six Sigma helps design things that don't break in the first place, things that do more and cost less. Further, both Six Sigma and Design for Six Sigma contain key factors that were absent in earlier quality movements, including a deployment strategy that works, a measurement system that managers care about (money!), and a balance between urgent, short-term projects and important, longer-term projects.

In a nutshell, things can get fixed in the short term with Six Sigma, and replaced in the long term with Design for Six Sigma innovations. (I use the somewhat flippant term *things* here to indicate the breadth of Six Sigma and DFSS initiatives, including the things an enterprise does to deliver the goods and services that customers truly want and need.)

One of the most obvious reasons for implementing Design for Six Sigma is that the Six Sigma improvement process usually cannot achieve Six Sigma performance by itself, as I've said earlier. Campaigns to improve existing products and processes encounter a barrier as they approach Five Sigma. Extreme efforts can sometimes push performance as high as 5.5 Sigma, but often such Herculean efforts encounter diminishing returns because their costs eventually threaten to consume any potential savings.

To exceed Five Sigma level of performance and cost effectiveness, organizations need fundamentally new design concepts. Using Robust Design® methods (which I'll describe in much more detail in Chapter 6), new designs can achieve incredible performance levels of Six Sigma and beyond—levels previously thought unattainable!—and do it all cost effectively.

Of course, not everything that companies do *needs* to achieve Seven or even Six Sigma performance levels. But for products such as airplanes and automobile tires, where achieving Six Sigma quality can literally be a matter of life and death, Design for Six Sigma comes to the rescue. It's also proving to be an invaluable asset for companies fighting for customers in highly competitive fields, including virtually all businesses making and servicing high-tech products, not to mention the burgeoning service economy, which must satisfy increasingly demanding customers better than the competition can. All these tasks are tough, and therefore ripe for DFSS projects.

While I believe the financial benefits DFSS can provide are clearly important, I feel the *sustainable* competitive advantages DFSS can create through rapid innovation are just as important, if not more so. In DFSS, the term *innovation* covers a lot more ground than the traditional perception. DFSS innovations can include new products, new processes, and new service concepts. Design for Six Sigma yields more innovative, higher quality, and lower cost designs than any other known methodology—clear proof that it's not just another rah-rah program—it creates real, fundamental, and lasting change.

For all the occasional caterwauling against corporations, we must remember that the standard of living for all people depends on the ability of our companies to perform well, and DFSS helps corporations do exactly that. The benefits of implementing Design for Six Sigma are enormous. So are the risks of not embracing DFSS.

So how can companies effectively *apply* Design for Six Sigma? If we take a look back at how it all began, the answer will become obvious.

In the late 1980s, Six Sigma was born in the manufacturing world to improve the manufacturing process. A few years later, the Manufacturing Process Improvement for Six Sigma levels of quality sprouted a related branch to help other divisions— including accounting, sales, and service—to achieve Six Sigma quality. This new branch of Six Sigma was termed Business Transactions for Six Sigma.

During the second half of the 1990s, Six Sigma exploded onto the U.S. business scene as a process improvement methodology frequently broken down into five phases: Define, Measure, Analyze, Improve, and Control—DMAIC, an acronym that has become synonymous with the Six Sigma moniker and one that can be applied to virtually any function of a corporation. Today Six Sigma's applications include Manufacturing Process, Business Transactions, and Product and Process Design for achieving Six Sigma quality levels.

Many training and consulting firms try to combine all these methodologies into one classroom package. But the one-size-fits-all approach doesn't fit anyone very well. Separating these methodologies in the categories above helps us dive more deeply into each one, and keeps us from burdening all the employees with the job of mastering a mesmerizing array of statistical tools that many of them simply don't need. When it comes to DFSS, tailor-made is the way to go. So the question of how to apply Six Sigma and DFSS can be easily answered: select the division you want to improve, and then pick the specific Six Sigma/DFSS program to improve it.

Which Comes First: Six Sigma or DFSS?

Although we've already discussed the differences between the two programs, the question of which methodology comes first crops up often. General Electric and other companies now see Six Sigma and Design for Six Sigma as fundamentally distinct initiatives. Famed former GE Chairman and CEO Jack Welch shares the now common view that GE should have started DFSS earlier. It might be instructive to speculate how much further ahead of its competition GE would have been if it had initiated Six Sigma and Design for Six Sigma at the same time to allow the many different divisions of GE to fulfill their particular needs simultaneously. In other words, Welch feels they could have brought in both the repairmen and the design engineers at the same time to fix existing situations as well as plan new problem-free designs for the future. Certainly, Jack Welch has learned from the mistake, and smart managers are learning from Jack Welch.

You can take the question to the next level: How much stronger would Western corporations be today if Six Sigma and DFSS had been launched as equal partners from the start? It's that possibility that we can now fulfill today, which is why we seek to promote the introduction of both Six Sigma and DFSS simultaneously as a tightly knit family of initiatives to capture the full power of Six Sigma. Again, it's simply the wisdom of hiring both repairmen and engineers at the same time to fix the company's current "machines" while also designing new, better running ones.

Every organization should consider tailoring Six Sigma and DFSS to maximize their effectiveness for its business. However Six Sigma is partitioned, defined, and deployed, it is vitally important to regard the elements as members of the Six Sigma family and treat them as strategic equals.

APPLICATIONS OF DFSS

Now let's take an overview of the application of Design for Six Sigma for each of the following three environments:

1. Business transactions

2. Manufacturing processes

3. Engineered products, including materials, hardware, and software

Business Transactions

Business transactions refer to both internal business processes and external services delivered to partners, suppliers, and customers. Looking at the first group, internal business transactions, I'll define them here as a series of actions or steps that are best represented by flowcharts—things like running a payroll program, completing employee evaluations, and calculating project budgets. Improvements here are normally achieved with the Six Sigma DMAIC methodology, which helps identify and eliminate unnecessary steps in such processes and improve the flow of information between employees and divisions along the way. Six Sigma's DMAIC methodology can also reduce or eliminate the root causes of errors and bad timing in the chain of events by ensuring that the information to be processed is accurate to start with, and gets passed on correctly to workers at the next step.

In short, for business transactions, Six Sigma's DMAIC methodology provides simplified, clean translations of information from division to division, from step to step, to make sure the person at the end of the chain is dealing with the same information the person at the beginning of the chain had intended to deliver. You might recall the old "telephone" game, in which one person makes a statement to another, who passes it down the line person by person until it reaches the end of the line. When the last person repeats what finally came down to him, it is always so far off the original statement that everyone erupts in laughter. That's exactly what happens in many corporate processes doing it the "old way." Six Sigma's DMAIC ensures that all the messages are passed on in an accurate, succinct, and timely manner.

Let's take a look at a simple example to see how it all works.

First, a project is *defined* to improve a particular transactional process, say, billing. Internal and external customers are identified and their needs are determined—or in DMAIC terminology, *measured*. Next, the group also measures the time variations and errors that occur while delivering the service—the standard deviation and error rates of the accuracy and timeliness of the billing process. After the glitches are quantified, *analysis* reveals the sources of variation—perhaps a faulty computer program, a bad procedures policy, or sluggish personnel. That step is followed by problem solving to reduce or eliminate the root cause to *improve* the process. After the improvements in the transactional process are verified to be true, they are implemented with *controls* to sustain the gains over time.

This DMAIC methodology of Define, Measure, Analyze, Improve, and Control yields major improvements with only modest investments. Most companies enjoy significant financial benefits just months after a project is completed. Because it leaves the basic design of the original process largely intact, it is not terribly disruptive to the company's or division's ongoing operations. But, the amount of improvement possible is inevitably limited—kind of like putting on new wallpaper in the house: the house looks nicer but the living space is still the same. Experience indicates that the best possible performance a company can hope to achieve with the DMAIC method is Five Sigma— surely a major step up for almost every company, but not the Six Sigma quality they desire.

DMAIC can produce impressive returns, but more thorough and lasting changes can be created with Design for Six Sigma, founded on Robust Design Optimization. In short, DFSS utilizes a process called IDDOV which is what DMAIC is to Six Sigma. It stands for Identify the opportunity for improvement, Define the requirements, Develop the concept, Optimize the design, and Verify it. (Please note that Chapters 4 to 7 later will explain each of the phases of IDDOV methodology in detail.) DFSS doesn't just fix the process, but *redesigns* the process on the drawing table and thus prevents problems from occurring in the first place. It is not simply applied to the *improve* phase near the end of the DMAIC methodology. It starts by *identifying* the project to be undertaken, then proceeds to rigorously *define* (customer) requirements to capture the Voice of the Customer and translate the language of the customer into the language of the company. The next phase of DFSS is to *develop* the concept for a process that can be *optimized* to become insensitive to sources of variation (thereby making it robust) under actual, real-life conditions. The optimized concept is then *verified* through trials and pilot runs, then implemented with appropriate controls to sustain the gains.

Let's look at the billing example again. In DFSS's IDDOV model, we'd first *identify* the need to redesign a clumsy, slow, inaccurate system. Then we'd *define* the requirements by asking the customers (in this case, that would include internal divisions, suppliers, partners) what it is they really want from our billing department. More legible invoices? Faster turnaround time? More "customer service" to answer questions? Then we'd *develop* a new process concept that will potentially solve the old problems and satisfy the well-understood customer requirements. Next, we'd *optimize* the process concept, debug it in advance by running it past all involved, then rework it before it's implemented. Finally, we'd *verify* that the optimized process does what we wanted it to do by quantifying its performance and also getting the reviews from our customers. And that's how IDDOV works.

In DFSS, services are considered external transactional processes. The role of DFSS in such cases is the same as it is for the internal business transactional processes previously discussed.

This IDDOV methodology bypasses the Measure and Analyze phases of DMAIC by creating a process that prevents problems and variations from emerging from the outset. Build it right the first time and you don't have to spend so much time measuring and analyzing its performance. It is the long sought after *authentic prevention* methodology that breaks the Five Sigma performance barrier to yield Six Sigma results and beyond.

While the investment in most DFSS projects is relatively small compared to the benefits, the IDDOV methodology can take longer to yield financial rewards. But when the money starts coming in, the high end is much higher, as you can see in Figure 1.1, which illustrates the typical return rates of DMAIC and IDDOV projects.

Figure 1.1 demonstrates how both DMAIC and IDDOV cost money in the early stages of the project, but the revenues from a Six Sigma DMAIC project soon steadily rise, then level out, while Design for Six Sigma's IDDOV takes longer to rise but rises more steeply and levels out at a higher plateau.

Manufacturing Processes

DFSS explicitly allows companies to simultaneously design both products and processes. In Quality Function Deployment (QFD), links are made between product designs and manufacturing process designs. The objective is to optimize the articulation

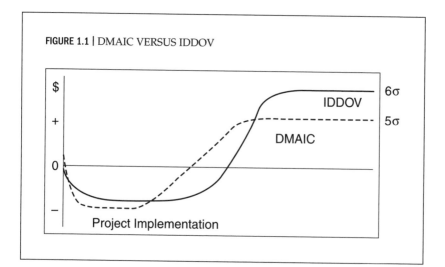

FIGURE 1.1 | DMAIC VERSUS IDDOV

between product designs and manufacturing process designs. In other words, QFD tries to get the architects and contractors working in concert to optimize the capability of the manufacturing process to consistently produce products with the highest quality, reliability, and customer satisfaction at the lowest possible cost.

DFSS is also a powerful methodology for improving or re-designing existing manufacturing processes. The DFSS tool box also includes *robust optimization* and *tolerance optimization* of the manufacturing process, mistake proofing, and design of real-time process controls and adjustments (including Control Charting, feed-back Control, feed-forward Control, and preventive maintenance—all of which will be defined in later chapters) to maintain manufacturing quality. It's the difference between making changes for an assembly line in an office far away and making them right on the assembly line while it's already in motion. DFSS is equipped to do it either way.

Engineered Products Including Materials, Hardware, and Software

DFSS makes most people think of engineering environments, and while we've already pointed out that it applies to far more than just engineering, engineering is in fact a popular target for Design for Six Sigma Projects. Product design is the other half of Concurrent Engineering, which entails integrating the development of both products and processes.

In such situations, Design for Six Sigma is normally implemented using Design of Experiments (DOE) for design optimization. DOE is a statistical process for tightening tolerances to reduce variation. It is equivalent to the Tolerance Design portion of Robust Engineering. While DOE is a valuable methodology with many applications, and may be the method of choice for optimizing transactional processes, it is not well suited for optimizing the functional performance of a system.

Engineered products are different. For engineered products, the objective is to optimize functional performance, not just reduce variability. In other words, the goal is not just to make the product as consistent as possible, but to make sure it can do the job it's designed to do well every time, on target every time. It's great to make 10,000 cars exactly the same with no variation whatsoever, but if the original design is poor and the car can only go 40 miles per hour, there's little value in knocking ourselves out to make 10,000 such cars exactly the same. Thus, optimizing functional (target) performance will minimize variability, but the converse does not necessarily always hold true. Minimizing variability may or may not optimize the product's functional performance. They are two very different goals. In golf, consistently hitting the ball out of bounds doesn't help the golfer achieve low score; consistently hitting the fairways and the greens does.

One crucial thought about engineered products is this: *functions before forms.* Customers may or may not realize this, but there is at least one energy transformation taking place behind every engineered product to fulfill the design intent (expected function). The customer can touch and feel the product; however, what it takes for the system to deliver the intended function is not always visible to the customer. For example, the function of a motor is to transform electrical energy into mechanical energy. The objective is to optimize the efficiency of the motor by maximizing the amount of energy created that flows directly to the motor shaft to make the golf cart, blender, or electric razor go. Making this transfer more efficient will subsequently reduce the amount of energy wasted on vibration, friction, heat, and noise that cause degradation of the performance, reliability, and the useful life of the electric motor. The "cleaner" the transfer, the better the product.

Japan's Dr. Genichi Taguchi's Robust Engineering method is the only known method that efficiently optimizes energy transformations to make products impervious to variations that occur in the environment and during actual usage. In other words, neither the weather nor bizarre customer operations of the product will affect its performance, just to name two easy examples.

The first step in Robust Engineering is to define the Ideal Function, a utopia where all of the energy flows into fulfilling the intended function of, say, the electric motor. When all energy goes toward fulfilling the intended function, there is none left over to cause wear and degradation of the machine. Of course, the Ideal Function is not achievable on earth, but it allows us to set the maximum performance against which real-world designs can be compared and measured—a true north we can use to see how close we can come to perfection.

Design of Experiments is not intended to optimize the physics of the function but it does generate statistics that are vital for Six Sigma's DMAIC methodologies. In addition, using statistical-based DOE allows us to use a common methodology for both product and process improvement. Needless to say, it's very helpful to be using the same "language," if you will, when we integrate the two.

As noted earlier, the one-method-fits-all approach is a major disservice to both engineers and businesspeople, because it doesn't fit either group well. Especially in the case of new product or process introduction, DFSS is the proper methodology because that's what DFSS is designed to attack: new products or processes. Six Sigma's DMAIC, on the other hand, focuses on improvement—which is largely useless with new products because there are not yet flaws that need to be improved upon. This also reinforces my earlier point that Six Sigma does not have to be a prerequisite for DFSS.

Product design is not simply a statistical process. It is an engineering process based on physics. Robust Design Optimization is an engineering methodology founded on physics. Boiled down, your choices look like this: Choose DOE for reducing variations in transactional processes and other appropriate circumstances. Use Robust Design for optimizing the performance of engineered products.

PART ONE

People Power of DFSS

CHAPTER 2

DFSS Implementation Strategy

Mao Tse-tung said the longest march begins with a single step. The point is, no matter how daunting the journey, the important thing is to get started.

In companies launching DFSS, however, it's just as important to make sure the first step is a good one—because if it's not, you might not get another one. With so many initiatives crashing upon companies in waves, year after year, employees are understandably suspicious of the latest push and weary of the endless revolutions.

That's why it's vital that a company's first DFSS Project must succeed or the organization will find itself unable to undertake any more initiatives any time soon thereafter. The program will be tagged with killer comments like, "We tried that before, and it didn't work. Remember?"

Therefore, it's important to pick a juicy target for your first DFSS Project, one that's sufficiently innovative to capture employees' imaginations—and avoid comments like "We're already doing that"—but straightforward enough to ensure that a solid effort will bring success, thus avoiding other cancerous comments like "It may work there but it won't work here." While flippant remarks can't kill a new initiative, the deeply rooted sentiments behind the comments can. It's best to nip them all in the bud by starting out strong.

Why has DFSS succeeded when other quality initiatives have failed? One reason is the involvement of such a large number of people in high places in the deployment and implementation phases of all elements of DFSS. The process starts at the top. When the other employees see that the CEO is on board, committed, and involved in DFSS, they'll be on board, too.

I'll show you how in this chapter, by walking you through a five-step deployment process that actually works. When it's implemented as described here, it will work for deploying both Six Sigma and DFSS initiatives, although we'll be focusing on the latter here, of course.

At first glance, the process may seem like any other deployment process. And in outline form, it basically is. But when I spell out how each of the five steps works in practice, critical differences will become clear.

These are the five steps for deploying a Six Sigma or DFSS initiative:

1. Executive management commitment

2. Education, training, and coaching

3. Effective communications

4. Integration strategy

5. Bottom-line performance

EXECUTIVE MANAGEMENT COMMITMENT

Executive management refers to the management team at the top of the organization consisting of the CEO and the corporate management committee or its equivalent in your company.

A new initiative can be seeded from within the organization or from the outside. Eventually, however, a new initiative must be *discovered* by those at the top of the house before it can become a viable corporate initiative. Following the discovery of an attractive initiative, the corporate management committee members must actively *decide* whether the initiative is right for their corporation—instead of just letting it happen.

As you might expect with any important decision, this can become a sticking point. Executives reporting to the CEO have many demands on their time, talent, and energy. Any new, unfamiliar initiative, no matter how successful at GE and elsewhere, is not something they will automatically embrace. And as I stated in Chapter 1, the word *design* often creates the misconception that the entire program is focused only on engineering, which causes executives to quickly conclude, "Oh, that is an engineering topic. Why don't we turn it over to the vice president of engineering?" Then they wash their hands of it.

This misconception must be corrected for DFSS to succeed. Design for Six Sigma has broad applications to all aspects of running a business, including internal business processes such as finance, human resources, legal, marketing, sales, service, manufacturing, and distribution, and even simple everyday concerns such as running a meeting and answering the telephone—not to mention, of course, engineering. Design for Six Sigma is simply a means of raising an organization to a new level of performance, and that applies to just about everything companies do.

CEO Commitment

Introducing any element of DFSS requires a major investment in both time and resources. Accordingly, it cannot succeed without the commitment and involvement of those at the top of the organization, right up to the board of directors. The CEO must visibly exude enthusiasm and unwavering commitment for everyone in his or her organization to see. Employees will rarely dedicate themselves to a new Project unless they see that the CEO believes in it, too, and demonstrates his enthusiasm publicly. There is no substitute for enthusiasm.

It's a simple point, perhaps, but one worth underscoring. As kids, we all knew from our parents' behavior what they really believed in and what they didn't—no matter what they told us. As they say, often our kids know us better than we know ourselves. And nothing affects our children's behavior more than our example. So it is with our employees. They know where to invest themselves, and where not to, based on the behavior the company's "top dogs" show them. Therefore, that's where DFSS starts—or ends.

To prove their commitment to DFSS to their employees, CEOs must put their time where their mouth is. Whether or not the company has already pursued other components of Six Sigma or DFSS, once the company decides to adopt Design for Six Sigma, the CEO must assume the role of the Chief DFSS Champion, the top job in the DFSS hierarchy, in addition to any other roles he or she has already assumed with Six Sigma or DFSS.

A rule of thumb about leadership: Don't expect your people to do anything you're not willing to do. There are few successful coaches who never played at the level of the sports they coach. They may or may not have been great athletes themselves, but they know what it is to make a pressure shot, to make a tackle, or try to hit a curve ball. And that's how they earn the respect and commitment of their players. That's how good executives do it, too.

If your company has already successfully launched the traditional Six Sigma program, it can obviously be a great boost to your organization's ability to adopt DFSS, too, because the employees will be familiar with the terms, the many roles, and the objectives of Six Sigma. But there can be different obstacles for an experienced company to overcome, too, when deploying DFSS.

Deploying the Design for Six Sigma program requires an enormous amount of change throughout the organization. Of course, despite what we all say, people generally do not like change. After all, they were rewarded under the old system, the way things have always been. A change represents a threat to their security and comfort level. So, any change any company tries to institute invariably generates advocates and adversaries within the organization, particularly among strong executives and managers who have succeeded in the previous company culture and are uncertain about their potential for personal success in the new, unknown culture.

The good news: Many of these employees will already have experienced the many benefits such changes can bring if they've been through Six Sigma. But those very same employees might be reluctant to go through some of those processes again. Taking on a second initiative such as Design for Six Sigma can seem overwhelming. Surprisingly, sometimes the strongest advocates of the first initiative can become the strongest adversaries of the second, especially if the first initiative is already succeeding in transforming the corporation and yielding financial benefits that meet or exceed expectations. What incentives do they have to leave a winner at mid-season?

Even if the original rollout plan that started a company on the Six Sigma system called for introducing Design for Six Sigma down the road, often employees develop significant resistance to its deployment. It's almost inevitable that you will hear them make suggestions to delay or even cancel the second initiative, DFSS.

Real change is a tough gig. Two big changes back to back is an even tougher gig. That's why it may be even more critical for the CEO to shine brightly as the Chief DFSS Champion to successfully deploy Design for Six Sigma than it was for the CEO when he or she successfully deployed Six Sigma. Without the unfailing support of the CEO, deployment of Design for Six Sigma can get bogged down in so much controversy so quickly that it can become almost completely ineffective in the crucial early stages. But it's imperative that we avoid these early troubles because, as you'll remember, any new DFSS initiative must succeed or the corporation will be shut out from that option for several years. In addition to demonstrating support by giving time, effort, presentations, and financial backing to DFSS, CEOs can show their enthusiasm simply by using the old "management by wandering around" technique, one of the most effective means available to show support.

Executive Management Committee Commitment

As I've stressed, when the CEO adopts the role of the Chief DFSS Champion, many of the early obstacles are quickly broken down. But even if the CEO's on board, some members of the executive management committee might balk. If a single member of the executive committee "blockades" the advance, the deployment process can crumble. Any crack in the dam of commitment sends a signal to others in the organization that top management isn't really serious about this new program and it's just a fad they will discard if enough people resist. This then becomes a license for other managers to set their own priorities, which almost certainly will entail doing what they were already doing before and giving the new, unfamiliar initiative lip service until it goes away like the others that preceded it.

That's why even a single dissenting vote or a hard-line position taken by just one strong member of the executive team needs to be addressed up front prior to proceeding with deployment. Every member of the executive management committee must buy in, at least enough so they can honestly say, "I will support and live with the decision to deploy this new initiative," and mean it. A close friend of mine had a great definition of the word *consensus*: "You have consensus when every member of the group can say, this is a decision I will *actively* support."

The best way to prevent cracks in the dam from starting is to give the members of the executive committee a thorough understanding of the new initiative by carefully covering what DFSS is, how it will help the enterprise as a whole, and, not least, how it will help them personally. Once they see the price for not participating and the potential gains for jumping on board—personally and professionally—getting their cooperation will naturally be that much easier.

Once the CEO and top executives are on the team, it's time to turn your attention to the third success factor: planning for a flawless rollout.

Planning for a Flawless Rollout

The executive team plans the rollout, which normally takes about three months of relatively intense activity. The outcomes of a good planning process include increased understanding of DFSS, especially what it takes to overcome the obstacles to a great initiative, and a rollout plan that reflects this newly gained wisdom.

In some ways, the planning process mimics the attributes of a Six Sigma–style deployment process—the very ones that make it succeed where other deployment efforts have often failed. The keys in both cases are: the focus on specific Projects, not just vague improvements; the involvement of a large number of Champions and Project Sponsors positioned throughout the organization; and the means to track the financial impact of Projects on the bottom line.

Because Design for Six Sigma strives for the flawless execution of business processes and the development of flawless products and services, it only makes sense that the rollout of the first DFSS initiative must meet the same standards to set the tone for the rest to come. First impressions create mind-sets that are very difficult to change. As they say, you don't get a second chance to make a first impression. If the first few months of the rollout of Design for Six Sigma proceed without significant problems, the Hawthorne Effect kicks in, in which any visible efforts to improve something by themselves will create improvements. In other words, organizations always get an initial boost from change for change's sake. Thus, when employees see that their company is making an honest, concerted effort to improve the organization, that by itself will have immediate benefits in morale, effort, and production.

The Hawthorne Effect's contrapositive, however, can be devastating. If the initiative stumbles out of the gate, not only will it cause the demise of the DFSS initiative, it will prompt everyone from the employees to the board members to discredit management for its apparent lack of judgment in introducing the initiative in the first place. Negative attitudes generated by the "Anti-Hawthorne Effect" can bring down the organization's performance to levels even lower than its original, pre-DFSS condition. Like a superbug that survives another round of pesticides, employee cynicism and resistance to all future changes will grow stronger. Future attempts to initiate change will be even more clearly perceived as fads that will fade away if ignored long enough. This phenomenon is very powerful and should be guarded against at almost all costs. Reintroduction of a failed initiative is virtually impossible. Clearly, for all these reasons and more, the first attempt at a DFSS Project must succeed.

By practicing change we become better at change, and can thereby eradicate the "Anti-Hawthorne" menace. As with everything else, practice makes perfect. Corporations that practice innovation and implementing change eventually get good at it. And likewise, those that have been slow to change over the years find change very difficult to implement. Corporations that constantly practice change can actually accelerate their *rate* of change to outpace their competition and win the race to lead the marketplace. Your goal is to help run one of those corporations.

EDUCATION, TRAINING, AND COACHING

It probably goes without saying that a new business initiative won't work without education, training, and coaching, but it's important to see all three as distinct parts of the process.

Education is largely a one-way communication effort, like a lecture (although a good trainer will always involve his or her audience). For DFSS education, your people will meet with a skilled trainer either on-site or at a meeting hall. Training occurs both externally and internally, where the experts *show* you how it works. In the coaching phase, the participants take the wheel and get accustomed to how it works by doing it themselves, but with an expert looking over their shoulders, giving them help when needed. Before long, they themselves will be able to take over some of the education, training, and coaching duties in their organizations.

Champions are the first to go through DFSS training, which is usually delivered during the three-month planning period. All Champions go through one week of training to learn the leadership, deployment, and technical skills needed to carry out their responsibilities—namely, fostering the deployment and implementation of DFSS. Because one of the first tasks Champions must perform is selecting a viable Project, the initial training focuses on Project Selection, in addition to how to project financial benefits and how to track progress against financial objectives.

Champions undergo their training prior to Project Selection and Black Belt training. (The Black Belts are the principal movers and shakers on DFSS Projects, and will be discussed in greater detail in the next chapter, as will all other roles and titles.) I also recommend that CEOs participate in the second round of training with Level 1 Champions to familiarize themselves with the program and also to demonstrate commitment. As I've said before, if the CEO is not on board, no one else will be. DFSS Black Belts must undergo rigorous training for four weeks spread over six to nine months and in between weeks of training, DFSS Master Black Belts provide coaching on the projects so that Black Belts apply their knowledge effectively on their projects. A common misconception is that if Six Sigma Black Belts take an extra week of DFSS training it will make them DFSS Black Belts. This is one of the major reasons why organizations are not getting substantial results on DFSS implementation. To be certified as a DFSS Black Belt, someone must effectively finish a DFSS project that may take up to a year to complete.

An important note: Even Six Sigma Champions who take on the additional responsibility of Design for Six Sigma need training in DFSS, because the two have some fundamental differences that must be grasped for the organization to be successful. For Project Sponsors, usually about one week of DFSS training is needed to get started. For Deployment Champions, two or three days of training may be adequate. Specialized training modules, if needed, are normally delivered toward the end of the planning cycle or early in the deployment cycle prior to finalizing Project selections.

Projects

The word *Project* is consistently capitalized here to make a point. Projects are a big deal in DFSS. Projects are the vehicles to get things done. My experience has shown that simply composing a list of "action items" never inspired anybody to do anything. Only when a dry, lifeless action item is transformed into a Project complete with resources, objectives, and plans to achieve them does any substantive task get accomplished. A list is just a list, but a Project plan is a call to action.

In the Six Sigma and Design for Six Sigma arenas, Charters are developed for possible Projects and are submitted to the selection committee. For the selected Projects, a Charter is refined into a well-defined Project plan containing six elements:

1. Project name and problem statement

2. Definition of scope

3. Identification of team members

4. Objectives

5. Schedules

6. Target for financial benefits

All Charters and Projects are cast into a standard form to help with communications, tracking, and comparisons. The idea is not to suck creativity out of the process, but to provide a consistent communications tool so the reader can immediately see what the Project is all about, and compare and contrast it with others.

Projects are at the center of all DFSS education, training, and coaching. They are the heart and soul of DFSS. How Projects are formulated and operated is one of the most critical aspects to ensuring the success in Six Sigma and Design for Six Sigma. For example, every Project's financial benefits (or goals) are baked into the Charter, which makes it easy to track the Project's progress accurately and demonstrate the flow of financial benefits to the corporate bottom line. Thus, Projects not only get things done, they also measure the benefits to the company in dollars and cents—something every boss likes to see, because such tracking is as valuable as it is rare.

The Deployment Champions, Project Sponsors, and Master Black Belts develop the Charter. Their first job is to determine the Project's scope—that is, what they will address and what they won't address. Defining the scope is one of the most critical and difficult steps. In much the same way a photographer determines how widely or narrowly to focus on her subject, the group must determine just how much it can bite off with the first Project. Bite off too little, and you inspire no one. Bite off too much, and you will set yourselves up for failure. (The latter, by the way, is much more common.) The work of determining the scope starts during Champion and Sponsor training and is completed with the end of Black Belt training.

Here's how the training works. On the first day, Black Belts—the leaders of the ground troops of DFSS—bring team members together to review a carefully defined Charter. After providing some basic background information on Design for Six Sigma, the Black Belts give the teams one or two hours to refine their Charters into Projects, including resources they will need, schedules they will follow, milestones and "inch-stones" they will achieve along the way, and how they plan to attain the targeted financial benefits. Because this is often the first time the team has had the opportunity to work together, the activity also serves as an icebreaker, and the first step toward team building.

In-class exercises are designed to allow the diverse team members to get together to actually *work* on their Project. The instructors become coaches during the exercise periods to help the teams when needed. This hands-on form of learning has proven to be very effective. As the old Chinese proverb states, "Tell me, I forget. Show me, I remember. Involve me, I understand." That's why DFSS training leans a lot more towards *show* and *involve* than *tell*.

In fact, coaching is a central element of all DFSS education and training phases. Classroom learning without on-the-job practice under the guidance of a mentor is virtually no learning at all. Coaching is a major portion of the investment in DFSS. Management is often tempted to reduce the cost of the program by reducing the number of coaching days, but this usually backfires. Well-coached Projects deliver larger financial returns sooner than those that have been short-changed on coaching days.

For Six Sigma, it's reasonable to expect Projects to be finished in about 6 months from the first day of training, and for investments in an outside consulting firm to be recovered within 12 months of initiation. But Design for Six Sigma Projects tend to

run a little longer, between 6 and 18 months, and returns are delayed until the new designs are implemented, perhaps up to two
years from the first day of training.

Management and team members alike often express the concern that too much emphasis on monetary benefits might distort
the behaviors of the team to focus only on quick financial gains
at the expense of lasting opportunities for change. While this is
a legitimate concern, surprisingly, it does not often arise in practice. After employees have some experience with the process, the
concern usually becomes negligible.

Of course, the integrity of the process depends on the behavior of the people judging the effort—the Champions and the
managers. If managers are excessively focused on managing
money rather than managing the activities that yield money,
Projects can get distorted. "Show me the money" may be a
catchy movie phrase, but such myopic thinking can be destruc-
tive for DFSS Projects if the focus is so strong it obscures everything else.

A major principle of Design for Six Sigma is to manage the
process effectively, not the immediate results—just as winning
football coaches do. A smart coach will be more pleased by a
well-played, close loss against a good opponent than a poorly
played, sloppy win over a bad one, because he knows that if his
team is playing well, the wins will take care of themselves over
time, and if they're not, the lucky victory probably can't be du-
plicated very often.

Focusing excessively on financial gains leads to shortcuts,
shoddy work, and ultimately disappointing outcomes. Pursuing
excellence in *how* the work gets done leads to superior performance over the long haul, and Projects help employees focus on
that brand of lasting excellence. Surprisingly, in some ways, it's
those people who claim to be the most bottom-line-focused
workers who typically have the most difficulty buying into Design for Six Sigma strategies. If they make demands for quick results, it will inevitably lead to expensive fire fighting down the

road to find and fix the mistakes that were baked into the Project months earlier. DFSS is not quite a marathon—a two-year turn-around time for fundamental change, strong, sustainable profits, and lasting success is not much to ask—but it's not a sprint, either. Keeping the right expectations in mind is vital to the success of DFSS.

Outside Consulting Leadership

A good outside consulting house, one that specializes in Design for Six Sigma and genuinely cares about its clients' success, can help begin the initiative by explaining what DFSS is to the CEO, the executives, and the other top decision makers involved, including how DFSS works, and what it has done for other companies and employees. Experts can weave a compelling story based on facts derived from their own experience about how the power of Design for Six Sigma transforms a corporation into a winning powerhouse, benefiting all who work for it.

Outside consulting is probably more critical to the success of Design for Six Sigma than it is for Six Sigma, for three reasons. First, it has the word *design* in it, which seems to mislead all who first encounter it that it's primarily an engineering initiative. Second, it is new and therefore has not been touted as broadly as Six Sigma—at least, not yet. Third, there are two fundamentally different approaches to DFSS. One is derived from the statistically based DMAIC process of Six Sigma, namely Design of Experiments. The other is firmly grounded in the one of the most respected design methodologies, the Taguchi Methods® for achieving Robust Design®. The strength of Taguchi Methods derives from its powerful engineering strategies.

For many applications, including important service transactions, business processes, and certain aspects of engineering and manufacturing, Design of Experiments may be the appropriate methodology to use. But it is not a chameleon that can transform itself to look like an engineering design optimization process, so it is necessarily limited, more so than some consultants would have you believe. Nevertheless, a good DFSS methodology should include both Taguchi Methods and DOE so that both are available to Project teams to be used as needed.

If the company's DFSS team is not fully versed in both methodologies, which will be explained in greater detail later in this book, the management team does not have the option to choose between them for different applications. The narrow approach of "my way or the highway" is not the best approach for the client. Most consulting firms push statistically based DOE wrapped in robustness to make it more saleable, but it's a ruse. You need both.

The duties of the outside consulting house naturally should also include initial training and insight about all of the elements of customer-focused DFSS initiatives, what is involved in deployment, and how strong leadership can help develop a flawless rollout plan.

EFFECTIVE COMMUNICATIONS

A baseball catcher tells the pitcher what pitch to throw by using just a few fingers. A baseball coach tells the batter to bunt, watch the pitch, or swing away through an elaborate series of signals. A football coach tells his quarterback what to do with a string of touching his cap, arm, and belt, not to mention a long list of coded commands for the huddle. "23 Skidoo" means nothing to us, but it signals a play to an NFL quarterback.

Getting the right signals to the right people at the right time is a vital task for any organization that plans to succeed. Everyone needs to know what the play is in order to execute it perfectly—and the key to all that, of course, is communication. Good communication is clear, consistent, and concise—and that's the goal of DFSS communications.

The DFSS communication plan is developed during the three-month planning for flawless rollout. GE provides a highly visible benchmark for implementation of Design for Six Sigma in general, and particularly with respect to how it communicates its plans to its employees. You will recall the brief but bold excerpts from the 1998, 1999, and 2000 annual reports mentioned in Chapter 1. In 1998, Jack Welch announced: "Every new product and service in the future will be DFSS—Designed for Six Sigma." Not much wiggle room in that statement. GE has consistently and clearly communicated not only its future plans to its employees, it has also confirmed and celebrated its successes along the way, which serves to strengthen employees' confidence in DFSS. The annual report is a very small portion of GE's total communications effort, but the sequence of annual reports exemplifies a consistent and clear message. It let the employees know the top management was so committed to the program to mention it in the annual report, and its commitment never wavered from year to year.

As defined by DFSS, communications are much more than podium speeches, fliers, memos, bulletins, banners, and so forth. These can all be effective means of communicating, but they're just wallpaper unless they're backed up by the behaviors necessary to make them all come true. In other words, the management team needs to "walk the talk." It's not enough, of course, simply to discuss or even plan a flawless rollout plan unless it is flawlessly *executed.*

If the need is great enough, many companies have discovered that appointing a Design for Six Sigma "communications czar" saves time and money while getting the message out more simply and effectively. The czar, like a good editor, can even circulate through the organization to talk with Champions and Project teams to find "stories" and issues to communicate to other DFSS people. This will serve to carry the message about the organization's commitment to DFSS as a corporatewide initiative, and help propel the enterprise into the future.

You might recall in the early days following the September 11, 2001, tragedy how difficult it was to determine the truth from the countless governmental press conferences, which often delivered conflicting information. After a few days of this, the government wisely coordinated its communications efforts to make sure the public was getting a consistent message. This also resulted in fewer press conferences but more accuracy—a win-win from the speakers' point of view, and probably that of the listeners as well. Remember this lesson when you begin to roll out DFSS.

However it's accomplished, the goal is the same for all DFSS organizations: Every individual throughout the entire organization should be receiving the same messages in consistent and clear terms. Champions and managers also need an "elevator speech" that they can deliver in less than three minutes about the whats, whys, and hows of Design for Six Sigma to any number of internal audiences, big or small. Further, DFSS brings with it a new vocabulary. It is the responsibility of all DFSS leaders to be able to explain what DFSS is about in terms that everyone will understand. The proof of your success is evident when the recipients of the message are able to pass the message on to others accurately.

Communicate Contents of Design for Six Sigma

The communication problem naturally expands when the entirety of DFSS is on the table, instead of just a component of it. Naturally, the more that's addressed, the more complicated the communication problem becomes.

DFSS covers a lot more than just the optimization of designs. It starts with sophisticated methods for gaining unique, in-depth understanding of the Voice of the Customer. It includes a detailed Quality Function Deployment to translate and propagate the Voice of the Customer throughout the Project development process. Once the customers' requirements are defined, the

DFSS team will move on to engage powerful methodologies for Concept Generation and Selection, including Theory of Inventive Problem Solving (TRIZ), Pugh's Concept Generation model, DOE, and Robust Design, not to mention a rich array of contemporary best practices to ensure that the new product and process designs deliver their full value to the customers.

Needless to say, not everyone in the organization will have a complete understanding of the many components described above—and that's why the DFSS communication team needs to be able to explain these concepts and answer questions for a wide variety of employees, from local experts to neophytes, and all those in between.

The communications team needs to be prepared to answer the following frequently asked questions:

- What is DFSS?

- What does optimization mean?

- What does it mean to translate the Voice of the Customer into the Voice of the Company?

- What is the operational definition of prevention in the DFSS model?

- How does variability of a business process translate into waste and cost?

Develop a "Crib Sheet"

The above questions are not easy to answer in just a few minutes. This is why the communications team should consider developing a "crib sheet" that explains the essence of DFSS and why it is important to the enterprise, to their organization, and to each employee personally, in short, easy-to-understand phrases. Such informational packages help the communications team convey a consistent and clear message that every individual can understand.

All of this may seem daunting at first glance. But far more quickly than you could imagine, provided you have proper communications support, the new DFSS vocabulary and concepts become clear, simple, and second nature to all your employees. When this happens, the power of DFSS becomes obvious. As with any productive learning situation, getting there is at least half the fun.

INTEGRATION STRATEGY

It's great when everyone is doing his or her job the correct way, with intelligence, passion, and commitment to the goals of DFSS and the company. It's a far greater thing, however, when everyone is doing his or her job *in concert* with everyone else. Integration is the key—the difference between a team of individual stars struggling to shine and a well-oiled machine unconcerned with personal glory as long as the team wins.

Two sets of activities need to be integrated into existing business processes. The first is the rollout of DFSS activities. Initially, the wide array of roles, the DFSS training process itself, and all ongoing Projects are overlaid on the company's existing practices. Over time, however, these elements need to be integrated into the company's continuing business-as-usual processes, or else they'll be sloughed off. The second set of activities that needs to be integrated is the new or improved processes and products created by DFSS Projects.

This may sound simple, but it is *crucial*. It's not enough to design a sophisticated artificial hip. If the body rejects it, you have nothing. The key is to make sure the body accepts it so it can do its job for years to come. Effective integration is what differentiates a high-powered, long-lasting strategic initiative from a fad. If the integration fails, the initiative will fade into obscurity and become just another used-up fad on the trash heap. If the integration succeeds, however, corporate performance will be elevated to unprecedented heights, and DFSS will be a living part of your organization.

Integration of DFSS Rollout

Transforming an initiative like DFSS into an ongoing, sustainable business process is central to maintaining and growing the gains after the outside consultants are gone and the initial roar of DFSS subsides into the background. The corporation needs to create an environment that fosters change and ensures the corporation's robustness against the chaos that change inevitably creates. All employees need to view constant improvement as part of their daily work. That means constantly watching for opportunities to improve, and speaking up when they find them. More specifically, they should be encouraged to identify potential Projects and seek out a DFSS "agent" to help formulate and submit the idea to the standing Project Selection Committee.

Two important factors of Design for Six Sigma's early success is the deliberate search for problems and opportunities for improvement and the mechanisms for formulating and selecting Projects. After the rollout is complete, the committees and functions put in place during the deployment of Design for Six Sigma need to be integrated into normal business operations as permanent entities. Otherwise progress will stop and some of the gains already made will be lost.

Likewise, the responsibilities for continuing the education, training, and coaching of the people filling the various DFSS roles can be taken over by the organization's education team or the quality team. When companies take over their own DFSS programs, they effectively make the shift from being given fish to learning how to fish.

But let's be clear about this: Don't neglect the coaching. It must be formally included as part of the package, or the employees will be as adrift as players without a sideline leader. Employees know who's committed, and who's on top of things, and they respond accordingly. Coaching must be formalized, planned, and funded. In short, it must be taken seriously.

Integrate New Processes into Existing Processes

Managing Design for Six Sigma when it's contained within DFSS Projects is relatively painless and simple. Integrating DFSS into an enterprise's New Product Development Process (NPDP) is quite a different challenge. It's the difference between working with a caged lion and a free-roaming one.

While the integration methodology is relatively straightforward, its implementation can consume substantial resources. A new NPDP has to be laid out in such a way that product and manufacturing engineers will actually use it rather than shelve it. This means software needs to be written, debugged, and deployed. Training materials need to be developed, and trainers need to be trained.

While integrating DFSS into the NPDP is straightforward, integrating new or modified transactional business processes into ongoing daily operations can be treacherous, similar to the challenge of modifying a vital computer system while it is still up and running in daily use. The solution, however, is similar too. The safest practice is to ensure the new system is debugged and fully operational prior to unplugging the old system. Even then, the new system often causes unexpected problems despite the fact that the integration was carried out by experts knowledgeable about the new system.

Adopting such a safe practice is even more difficult in core business processes such as purchase orders or payroll. Transactional business processes tend to be staffed with clerks and professionals that understand their own portion of the process but are certainly not experts at changing the overall system, or very experienced at adapting to new processes. Therefore, the people in charge of DFSS in your company must strive to become the experts about both the old and the new processes.

Both Six Sigma and Design for Six Sigma recommend that trials or pilots be conducted to ensure the fewest possible "translation" problems during the transition. This means that before the switch is made, employees need to document the new process, develop the training materials, and teach the clerks and professionals how to use the new system. Then, under the guidance of the internal DFSS experts, the group can transfer its old operations to the new system.

While all of this does not need to be spelled out word for word, the transition process needs to be documented and standardized at least to the level of guidelines. A major challenge with business systems is that they are often replicated at multiple sites around the world. A replication methodology should be developed that is both standardized and flexible at the same time, a challenging requirement in itself. It is, as the Jesuits would say, a classic case of "freedom within discipline." Let the transition teams around the world know what is nonnegotiable, and leave the rest to their creative minds to resolve in their own way.

I spell all this out to emphasize that integrating these processes is vital to the success of DFSS and the success of the company itself, and to point out that it does not just happen by snapping your fingers. An integration strategy must be planned and implemented as a separate, distinct function to facilitate rapid change and growth.

BOTTOM-LINE PERFORMANCE

As previously emphasized, tying Projects to bottom-line performance is central to driving the corporate culture change that has to occur whenever you're implementing a major new initiative. It is a big reason why Six Sigma and Design for Six Sigma have succeeded where other initiatives have not.

Total Quality Management (TQM) helped many companies enjoy significant improvements in bottom-line performance, but improvements achieved with TQM were difficult, if not impossible, to distinguish from the improvements other components generated. In other words, companies could tell they were scoring more points, but they couldn't be sure who was doing the scoring. Funding of TQM activities was founded on faith more than facts because returns on the investments were largely unknown.

The Six Sigma style solves this problem by first projecting how much you have to invest and what might be the likely returns on these investments up front, as part of the Project identification and selection process, and then tracking the outcomes all the way to the bottom line. This changes the psychology of decision making entirely.

As a result, the decision process shifts from faith-based hope to fact-based expectations. Favorable bottom-line results foster the search for new opportunities rather than debates about which, if any, additional investments should be made. Linking Projects to bottom-line performance is the catalyst for a constant, purposeful effort, year after year—the engine that transforms fads into lasting corporate changes.

Companies wise enough to make Design for Six Sigma a top priority enjoy the rewards of quantifiable financial benefits for years and years. Just ask Jack Welch.

CHAPTER 3

People Roles in DFSS

One of the most important elements of DFSS is the roles everyone plays. This is the *People Power* side of the equation. Any good football coach will tell you the same thing: Every player must have a specific role, clearly defined, with consequences for not coming through and rewards for doing his particular job well. And that goes for everyone in the organization, from the quarterback to the waterboys.

Same for DFSS corporations. The list of roles for DFSS Projects typically includes:

- Executive Leadership

- Champion

- Master Black Belt

- Black Belt

- Green Belt

- Team Member

Of course, it's not mandated that each organization fills all these jobs, or defines them in exactly the same way. Each company needs to tailor these to its own needs. I'll define each role, including the recommended training for each, and you can decide for yourself how you want to apply them in your company.

EXECUTIVE LEADERSHIP

In DFSS, you've got to have the Executive Leadership on board, the same way you have to get the owner of a football team on board before the team is going to go anywhere. The Executive Leadership has to be the driving force behind adopting the DFSS philosophy and inspiring the organization from Day One. If he or she doesn't want to do what's necessary to win, the team won't either. Likewise, if the CEO and his or her minions aren't behind the DFSS initiative or don't understand how it works, it won't fly. But if they get it and back it, everyone else will make a go of it.

The pace of DFSS Projects is influenced greatly by how often the Executive Leadership meets to address the DFSS initiative. The most successful DFSS companies meet monthly. Anything less seems to court delays and sluggishness, which naturally reduces the sense of urgency on which DFSS teams thrive. Better to have shorter, more frequent meetings than wait months for a marathon session.

In addition to the intangible duties of being the "spiritual leaders" of the DFSS initiative, the Executive Leadership has several important tasks—especially in planning and marketing—that must be done well for the Projects to succeed. Specifically, the Leadership Group must do the following:

- Establish the ground specific rules of the DFSS initiative.

- Select the area for Projects and provide the necessary resources.

- Review the progress of Projects periodically to instill accountability, provide guidance, and cut "red tape."

- Help calculate the Project's impact on the bottom line.

- Share best practices with other divisions, key suppliers, and customers.

A good CEO will likely appoint one of his or her executives to oversee and support the entire mission. This sends the signal to everyone else that the company is serious. It might be a vice president or a director of manufacturing or marketing, somebody who's highly visible and has pull. And that executive is called the Executive Champion.

The Executive Champion acts as the general, picking his personnel with great care, instead of assigning the office deadweight to a dead-end task. The people working on a DFSS Project are usually the most valuable people in the corporation, not the least valuable. When it's time for the Executive Champion, for example, to pick the Deployment Champions and the Project Champions, he or she picks from one of the highest levels of the corporation.

Although a DFSS Project is run primarily by the Black Belts in the middle of the company hierarchy, if they're not supported by the top leaders, that Project is not going anywhere. If the top executives don't take the time to learn about DFSS or support it, the Project leaders don't stand a chance. Any Project without that kind of backing is a Project that's set up for failure.

Almost everyone has been put in charge of a few of those Projects, and they almost always result in resentment. Few things aggravate employees more than knocking themselves out for the latest initiative, only to discover that the guys who had assigned it didn't care or notice if they had come through or not.

Almost everyone's been put in that position, and no one goes away feeling good about it. The top brass feels like the programs are a waste of time and money, the Project leader feels like he's been left to twist in the wind—or worse, set up as the fall guy—and the customers don't receive any benefit at all. All they notice is higher prices and a demoralized, fatigued service staff.

CHAMPION

As we've said, one of the CEO's first and most important tasks is appointing a full-time Executive Champion who will be responsible for overseeing and fostering the deployment of Design for Six Sigma. The Executive Champion is the leader of the Champion Team, with lower-ranking Champions answering to the Executive Champion from their posts within every major department within the enterprise. The Champions are among the first to be trained to deploy and implement Design for Six Sigma. Think of them as DFSS department heads, and you've got the idea.

Every business area, group, and department is expected to have a Champion reporting directly to that division's leader. The Executive Champion must have a strong role in selecting Champions because, after all, they're the ones who will make sure the ball keeps rolling. The intent is to fill the organization with Champions who are knowledgeable and passionate about DFSS—not to mention loyal to the Executive Champion's vision. It's the same with a football team, where the head coach has to be the one who picks his assistant coaches, because he must be assured that they're committed to him and see the game the same way. Having someone else pick his assistants is asking for trouble. From the Champions, the message spreads to the troops.

Champions implement DFSS within their divisions. They are responsible for identifying Projects, allocating the finances to get it done, and breaking down barriers. Naturally, the job is sufficiently important that the Champion should be selected from among the company's most prominent leaders. Higher-level Champions should be culled from the ranks of vice president and above, while even the lowest-level Champions should come from the group of directors, line managers, and executives within their divisions. All must exude a passion for excellence and customer satisfaction.

In traditional Six Sigma, the hierarchy of Champions goes as follows:

Executive Champion	Level 1	CEO
Deployment Champion	Level 2	President/
		Corporate Executive
Deployment Champion	Level 3	Vice President/
		Division Executive
Project Champion	Level 4	Director

The depth of the hierarchy of Champions obviously varies depending on the size and structure of the organization.

Like all management positions, the role of Champion requires perfecting the tricky balance between providing the team members the autonomy to make their own decisions and giving them the guidance they'll need to direct their efforts. Their responsibilities include:

- Setting goals for the DFSS Projects consistent with the company's priorities; this is assured by applying the DFSS Project Selection Screening

- Providing coaching on the Project, as needed, and approving changes in the scope or direction of the Project

- Finding (or negotiating) the resources needed to pursue the Project

- Representing the team to the Leadership Group and other teams, to advocate for the team, and smooth out any issues that arise among them

- Working as the Process Owners (more on that later) to ensure a smooth hand-off at the end of a DFSS Project

This is a rigorous list. But of all the items on it, providing coaching on the Project and approving changes in the scope or direction of the Project is probably the most important because frequently Projects slow down or stall because the Team Leader and the group are too reluctant to narrow the focus of the

Project—or shift it—because of their overwhelming fear of disappointing the Executive Leaders.

But it's far better to do one thing well than ten things poorly. Almost always, once a team is immersed in a Project, it discovers that the Project is more complex and involved than the Team Members first thought—and, therefore, narrowing the Project down becomes more important. The team should have the freedom to do this without the fear of being seen as "lightweights" by the company brass. A strong Sponsor can pave the way for them to do so without retribution.

The Deployment and Project Champions oversee the Black Belts under them and their Projects. They help the Black Belts by breaking down corporate barriers, creating support systems, and making sure the money is available to get the job done. They also help the Black Belts pick their improvement Projects, size up what the organization can do, and benchmark the organization's products and services. The bottom line is that the Deployment and Project Champions choose, evaluate, and support the Black Belts throughout their Projects. They're the foundation for success, without which the whole thing is bound to fail. And that's why smart Executive Champions pick the cream of the crop to perform these jobs.

The Project Champion's job is to oversee, support, and fund the DFSS Projects and the personnel necessary to get the job done. This allows the people on the Project to focus solely on the Project at hand.

This solves a common problem. Almost everyone can remember too many times getting an assignment from one guru, while still having to finish all his or her usual duties. As a result, neither Project is done well. The employee is pulled in two directions—unsuccessful at both. In the end, he or she often is forced to put the new assignment aside and return to performing the everyday tasks. And that's exactly why we need Champions to clear the tracks for the Project managers. The Champion often also serves as the Process Owner—that is, the person who receives the hand-off from the DFSS team upon the Project's completion and becomes the owner of the new or newly designed process. This requires assuming the responsibility to manage an end-to-end set of steps to provide value to an internal or external customer. This usually requires a cross-functional approach to the task.

With the introduction of Design for Six Sigma, you'll find that each Project needs increasingly diversified Champions, including Design Champions, Transactional Champions, and Process Champions—much as an increasingly sophisticated company needs more specialists to make it run well. In this model, some organizations might have two Executive Champions, such as a Six Sigma Executive Champion and a DFSS Executive Champion. Some divisions such as engineering or manufacturing might even have three Champions: a DFSS Champion, a Manufacturing Process Champion, and a Transactional Champion with a service background.

Project Champions are generally specialists. The skills needed by an Engineering Project Champion are obviously quite different from the skills needed by a Project Champion in, say, finance. At higher levels, executive responsibilities tend to span across a broad range of disciplines including marketing, engineering, manufacturing, finance, and so on. Such Champions could also be identified as Business Champions.

The football team model applies here as well. If you think of the CEO as the team owner, and the Executive Champion as the head coach, the divisional Champions would be equivalent to the offensive and defensive coordinators, while the Project Champions would be the position coaches, the guys whose job it is to work solely with the quarterbacks or receivers or linemen. At each level there is both support and accountability from above and below.

I advise you to maintain the traditional Six Sigma identities of Deployment Champions and Project Champions, but don't neglect the differences among them. You can, of course, call them whatever you wish—after all, a rose is still a rose by any other name—as long as it's clear that different Champions need different skills and different training to fulfill their different responsibilities.

The Deployment Champions are leaders who are assigned to devote their entire workday to managing the DFSS deployment and overlooking DFSS Project executions to which they've been named. On the other hand, a Project Champion is the owner of a DFSS Project and he or she is responsible for providing direct support to Black Belts who execute the DFSS Project.

The details of appointing Champions, deciding on titles, laying out training for the Champions, Master Black Belts, Black Belts, and Green Belts, performing Project selection, and rolling out the total Design for Six Sigma initiative were addressed in Chapter 2 in the section on Planning for a Flawless Rollout. As they say, God is in the details. In this case, the flawlessness of the plan depends on the flawlessness of the details. Using the principles of Design for Six Sigma to plan the rollout makes the rollout robust against sources of problems downstream.

MASTER BLACK BELT

A Master Black Belt (MBB) is an individual selected by a Champion to become an in-house expert for implementing DFSS, leading larger Projects, and training and coaching Black Belts. Master Black Belts occupy positions parallel to Deployment Champions. As in-house Master Black Belts are developed, the outside consulting firm turns more responsibilities over to the in-house Master Black Belts, and fades away from the picture.

Two approaches for developing and using Master Black Belts have emerged within Six Sigma. The first is to appoint and train Master Black Belts from the outset, at the same time the company selects the Champions. In this approach, MBBs go through Champion training and key elements of Black Belt training. Over time they go through additional training and experiences to develop technical and people skills beyond what is expected of Black Belts.

The second approach entails first training Black Belts for a few Projects, *then* selecting individuals from that seasoned batch of candidates to become Master Black Belts. For Design for Six Sigma, the second approach is preferred.

Here's a story to illustrate how it all works. When the CEO of a major conglomerate decided to introduce Six Sigma, he asked all of his managers to make a list of the people who might be able to replace them if they were to get sick or die suddenly. Because the CEO had a brush with death, being replaced was on his mind. The managers came back with lists of their top people and the CEO tabbed these stars to run the Projects. This action told the managers, more than anything, that the CEO was serious about DFSS and helped ensure its success.

When a company first decides to go with DFSS, the roles of Master Black Belts are played by outside consultants who come in as in-house experts on DFSS to teach the core points of DFSS to Black Belt candidates throughout the company. At the top end, they help the Champions select good Projects and the people to run them. Then they train and coach the people who will be doing the day-to-day work of DFSS and reporting the company's progress on the Projects. The Master Black Belts are the people most responsible for creating lasting, fundamental changes in the way the company operates from top to bottom. To do all that, the Master Black Belts must have the ability to pick the right Projects and the right people and teach, coach, and monitor them.

That's a lot to do, of course, which is why the outside consultants do the job at first. But when the people they've trained are ready, they assume the jobs of Master Black Belts from the consultants. That's right: the consultants' job is to make themselves obsolete!

To sum it up: The Master Black Belt works with the Champions to select the Project and the people who are going to work on it. Then they train and coach those people to succeed. The most important person they pick, though, is the Black Belt.

BLACK BELT

The Black Belts are the people who really do the work. They act as the fulcrum that supports the whole Project—the true leaders of DFSS. The biggest mistake a company can make is naming an employee who's not committed to be a Black Belt. That can virtually guarantee the failure of DFSS.

To ensure the success of the Black Belt, first you need to begin with a person who has considerable intellect and drive, and is willing to think outside the box. Black Belts must have both management and technical skills—a mix not everyone possesses—and the ability to inspire passion in front-line employees and confidence in the top brass. The most important thing a Black Belt does, though, is transform the DFSS vision into reality. They put the rubber to the road.

You might think it's difficult to find all those qualities in one employee—and obviously it's impossible to find the perfect Black Belt—but you will likely find that your company has a whole pool of talented folks waiting to be recognized, looking for an opportunity to test themselves and make a difference. It is a much bigger pool than most executives think they have. And talented, ambitious people don't usually savor the idea of spending their careers in second gear.

Once they're picked, the Black Belts have to help get funding for the Project, so they have to decide where to put their resources. Executive Leaders and Champions worry about *what* gets done, while Master Black Belts and Black Belts focus on *how* to get it done. And in the process they strive to achieve goals they never thought possible. But they are possible. In traditional Six Sigma, for a midsize to large corporation, a new Black Belt can save the company $200,000 to $250,000 per Project. Multiply that by four to six Projects annually, and savings from $800,000 to over $1.5 million a year become possible. In DFSS, these numbers are significantly bigger. Typically, one DFSS Black Belt project may contribute up to $1 million in the bottom line. When applying DFSS during a new product introduction, the organization may capture significant market share compared to a competitor who is not a DFSS devotee.

Now, how do you identify these superheroes? Fortunately, from experience, we know a few things about where to look. We've learned it's helpful to find someone who's already familiar with the company, but possibly frustrated by the company's old approach. Managers with a technical background seem to do better than others, too. Having said that, rookies can sometime bring a boldness to the Project that goes a long way. If you have the numbers, a mix of the two is often quite effective, for obvious reasons.

The length of service for a Black Belt depends on many things, but generally Black Belts are most effective when they're in the role for at least two years but not more than three—long enough to learn the job, but not so long they get bored or burned out by the Projects.

After you've picked the best candidates to become Black Belts, you need to train these superheroes. The most intense training focuses on DFSS Black Belts who will lead the Projects that actually deliver financial benefits to the organization. They receive the core DFSS education, training, and coaching. Classroom education and training is conducted in one-week sessions spread over a four-month to six-month period, depending on the Project's scope and complexity. Between training weeks, the Black Belts lead their teams on their Projects under the guidance of coaches (external Master Black Belts) who are initially provided by the outside consulting firm.

More specifically, after each week of training, the Black Belts go back to the workplace and put into practice what they've just learned. While it might be faster just to have them take all four weeks of training in succession, it would be less effective. Again, as the old proverb says: "Tell me, I forget. Show me, I remember. Involve me, I understand." When people get to practice what they've learned, it sinks in better. They get it. This way they can see it work, and they don't become brain-dead through non-stop training. And along the way, they start saving the company money immediately, because they're already trying out on their first Project what they've learned.

So, what do they learn? There are four core phases of the training, which match the four main points of the DFSS strategy: how to Identify and Define, Develop, Optimize, and Verify the processes that produce increased customer satisfaction, company savings, and a healthier bottom line. Those four topics are composed of things like engineering and process strategy tools such as Quality Function Deployment, Robust Design®, statistics, quantitative benchmarking, and Design of Experiments.

Some managers will already know some of those things, but almost no one knows all of them. More important, few, if any, will know how to apply all of these to DFSS Projects.

Let's compare DFSS training to the countless training courses employees have had to endure. Generally, employees have to sit down for a few days, while someone at the front of the room fills their heads with an endless stream of information—most of it either obvious or incomprehensible. Then they go back to their jobs, a few days behind, but no smarter.

We call those kinds of courses Data Dumps, in which the instructor just unloads his overheads on you and doesn't know or care if it sinks in or if you get it or not. But with DFSS you break down the Black Belt training into four parts, and after each training session, you go back and apply what you've learned. That way you remember it, but also, you have a lot more incentive to learn when you're in class.

We are aware that the prospect of a week of class for a new program is everyone's worst nightmare. But you can get past that by asking the designated employees if they're ready to start the first step of their DFSS Project. They will likely respond with the question: What was that first step again? But when they know they're going to apply what they learn a week later and be accountable for it, that changes everything. They want to learn, they want the help. And once they're in class, they realize DFSS teaches some familiar topics in unfamiliar ways. Everything they learn is geared to be applied specifically for DFSS.

The future Black Belts spend one week on the first subject, how to Identify and Define, then return to the workplace to try out what they've learned on a specific Project before coming back for the second week of class to learn the second subject, and so on. You can appreciate by now why the Black Belt is the most important link in the chain. While the success of DFSS depends heavily on the support of the Executive Champion, it's the guy in the middle who makes the whole thing spin.

Many people are surprised that anybody would give a mid-level person that kind of responsibility, that kind of power. But the Black Belts and the Master Black Belts are the only people in the chain who work full time on the DFSS Project, and *only* the DFSS Project. Remember: The Executives and the Champions might decide what gets done, but the Master Black Belts and Black Belts are the ones who figure out how to get it done.

So why would they give a middle manager that much authority?

Simple. It's like General Patton said: "Never tell people how to do things. Tell them what you want done and they will surprise you with their ingenuity in getting there." In other words, the more authority you give them, the more creativity and energy you get out of them. If something's your baby, and you'll get the credit or blame for it, clearly, you'll work a lot harder. However, there is little incentive to participate if you're a member of a committee of which no one's really in control or accountable for the group's success or failure.

But the biggest things a Black Belt gets are structure and tools: the structure to know what to do and when, with deadlines and numerical goals in place, and the statistical tools to analyze how they're doing and what needs to be done next.

It may sound like a lot of pressure, and in some ways it is. But being a Project manager—a Black Belt—also gives you a lot of visibility, a lot of credibility. It makes it fun to come to work when you've got so much power and responsibility.

This is no small benefit in an era when most employees can't remember the last time it seemed fun to go to work in the morning because it seems like their jobs consist mainly of a lot of pointless, anonymous busywork, with no end in sight. For most of them, they would happily take on some more responsibility if it comes with some excitement.

Another discovery: people seem to like the structure, the plan of attack, the numerical goals, and the specific roles that DFSS offers. A man we know once taught a seminar in which he asked the 20 participants how many of them had bosses who truly valued them and wouldn't want to lose them, and only one raised her hand! The most common complaint we've heard from dissatisfied employees is not low pay, long hours, or a hectic schedule, but this: they don't know what their bosses want, and no one appreciates what they do.

DFSS eliminates a lot of that because there's no question as to what's expected of you, when, and why. And because of all that accountability, there's no mistaking just what every member of the team has accomplished when a Project is completed.

GREEN BELT

The Green Belts provide the support the Black Belts need to get the Project done. They're trained in DFSS, so everyone is speaking the same language and is working for the same goals. That's the power of Six Sigma or DFSS: It's the first management philosophy that runs top to bottom, so everyone's on the same page. Further, the Green Belts can work themselves up to Black Belts if they do well.

The Black Belts aren't threatened by this because they are the ones who train the Green Belts and direct their efforts, and when the Green Belts get promoted, the best Black Belts move up to Master Black Belts—and the best of those, in turn, move up to Champions and eventually Executives. In fact, Jack Welch himself told his employees straight up that if they wanted to get promoted, they'd better be Black Belts.

Green Belts can be part-time or full-time members of the DFSS team. They are Project Team Members with some training in Design for Six Sigma. They are trained by the Black Belts, and receive about half as many days of training as the Black Belts. As anyone who's taught can tell you, teaching is one of the best ways to learn. This cascade of training further improves the Black Belts' understanding of DFSS and fosters team building. People outside the team may occasionally be identified as Resource Members for their special expertise or capability that might be needed by the team, but are not required to take any specific training.

TEAM MEMBER

The Team Members are simply those who help the Green and Black Belts pursue the Project with technical, managerial, or analytical support. They also help spread the word about DFSS tools and processes throughout the company, and become part of the reserve corps for future Projects.

The list of DFSS devotees reads like a who's who of the Fortune 500: General Electric, AlliedSignal, Caterpillar, Delphi Automotive Systems, Dow Chemical, and Ford, among others. But the biggest early convert was undoubtedly General Electric's CEO Jack Welch. In 1995, GE's operating margin was about 13.5 percent. By 1998, the company had raised it to 16.7 percent—a number Welch previously thought was impossible. That represents a $600 million bonus to the bottom line. Given these numbers, you probably can understand why Welch himself called Six Sigma and DFSS the most important initiatives GE has ever undertaken.

PUTTING PEOPLE POWER INTO PRACTICE

Every American company that hopes to survive, and even thrive, must question how it does business, and take nothing for granted. It's no longer enough to say, Hey, we've done it this way for 20 years. Twenty years ago almost no one had a personal computer, cable TV, or a CD player. Things have changed!

Things change and we have to change, too. This means we have to let go of some bad habits. One of them is ignoring the customers and the employees who serve them. They see and hear things people in the office don't. They know why a machine malfunctions; they know why customers are upset. They also know how to fix the machine and make the customer happy again—if we give them what they need.

One of the first things DFSS devotees do is pick several employees to become Black Belts. Unfortunately, instead of being excited, most of them think it is the kiss of death. And, perhaps, for good reason. Too many employees remember how these things used to go. When the top brass jammed a new quality program down your throat, you picked someone you could afford to miss for a few weeks to run the show.

If you've been on both sides of that equation—the dumper and the dumpee—you understand that neither side is much fun. We can all remember hoping to be overlooked for such exalted posts.

What starts to change their minds is when the boss calls them into his or her office and explains exactly what's going on. When a boss explains that the entire organization is committed to this, including the top brass—or the Executive Leadership, as we call it, and the Deployment Champion—and that he or she has studied the program carefully and even conducted a fairly lengthy search for people to run some of the most critical Projects—the Black Belts—people put aside their doubts and get on board. And when the boss explains that the Black Belts are going to receive a four-week training program, spread out over four to six months at a cost of some $15,000 to the division, it will get their attention!

PART TWO

Process
Power
of DFSS:
IDDOV

C H A P T E R 4

Identify and Define Opportunity

The purpose of Phase I of DFSS, the "ID" of IDDOV—Identifying the Project and Defining the Opportunity—is to provide strong, clear directions for the efforts to come. Because all future activities of the Project will build on the foundations established in this phase, its importance cannot be overemphasized. A small mistake here will have ripple effects and grow into ugly results down the road, like kinking the branch of a sapling to watch it become a deformed arm of an otherwise mighty oak. Care must be taken to do the job right, from the outset.

The two primary objectives for Phase I are:

1. Get the project started on the right foot.

2. Clearly define the requirements for which the team is aiming.

DFSS PHASE I/PART 1 (IDENTIFY) OVERVIEW

Here is an overview of DFSS Phase I/Part 1, and the activities it entails:

- Approve team project charter.

- Create business case.

- Complete project plan.

- Determine customer needs (with QFD).

- Prioritize customer needs.

- Define product requirements and targets (with QFD).

- Identify Critical to Quality (CTQ) measures.

The objectives in Phase I include developing a Project charter that will focus the Project's purpose and scope, producing a solid business case of the Project, and creating a detailed Project plan. Together, the Project charter, business case, and Project plan will serve in concert as the contract between the team, the sponsor, and the company itself.

Another key objective of Phase I is mastering a powerful method for translating the Voice of the Customer into the design requirements, namely Quality Function Deployment, or QFD.

Each deliverable from this phase requires input from market research and final management approval before the team can move forward. It is especially important to get approval for the team charter, the business case, and the requirements derived from the Voice of the Customer (VOC), as these constitute the very core of Phase I and from them the entire program is built.

After the Project charter, business case and Project plan are completed and approved, the team will work to establish the set of product requirements. These requirements will be based on the Voice of the Customer and contain the aspects deemed most Critical to Quality (CTQ) for the product or process in pursuit. They will be thoroughly documented to enable and support the subsequent phases in DFSS.

Quality Function Deployment will serve as the primary methodology for capturing and prioritizing the Voice of the Customer and then transforming it into product requirements.

Let's start from the top with a look at the DFSS project charter.

DFSS Project Charter

The breakdown of the DFSS Project charter encompasses:

- Project objective and goals

- Project scope

- Project milestones

- Project budget

In preparation for the charter for the Design for Six Sigma Project, you must answer the following questions:

- What are the overall objectives and goals of the Project?

- How big is the Project and what resources will be committed to it?

- What are the key deliverables and when are they due?

- What should we expect to spend and on what to accomplish our objectives?

By addressing these issues from the outset in concrete terms, you will be prepared to focus on the Project's intent: designing a product or process that achieves the previously unattainable Six Sigma level of quality. If you do this initial phase with diligence, you'll be on your way to achieving exactly that.

A DFSS Project charter is an important but simple document. Let's break down the list of the DFSS Project charter template point by point (see Figure 4.1).

Assuming you know how to name your own Project, we'll move right on to objectives and goals.

Strategic objectives and goals. The objective of your project should be to create a new Six Sigma product or process

- within budget,

- on schedule, and

- at the required quality level.

When determining your objectives, there are two critical points to consider. Should you

1. upgrade an existing product or process to a Six Sigma level of quality, or

2. modify an existing product or process for a new market?

FIGURE 4.1 | DFSS PROJECT CHARTER TEMPLATE

Project Name:

Project Objectives and Goals:

Project Scope:

Project Milestones and Budgets:

One of the central tenets of a DFSS Project, and one that distinguishes it from a Six Sigma Project, is that the goals tend to focus more on long-term results, which is exactly what the DFSS tools and methods are designed to produce. For example, the group might strive to create a new DFSS product that will have vastly improved scores for customer satisfaction. The improved satisfaction will then lead to increased market share, which does not occur overnight with quick fixes. DFSS provides the framework to meet goals that will provide lasting gains for the company for years to come.

As with virtually everything in the DFSS system, this applies not only to DFSS products, but also to processes, such as those that might reduce long-term costs like waste or payouts for service and warranty contracts.

DFSS Project objectives and goals. The five keys to determining the DFSS Project's objectives and goals are as follows:

1. Improve customer satisfaction (and/or market share).

2. Improve profits (and/or profit margin).

3. Reduce customer complaints (and/or service costs).

4. Reduce waste (and/or improve efficiency).

5. Develop robust technology applicable for family and future products.

It probably goes without saying that establishing objectives and goals does many good things for any group working together, including giving the group a mission, a focus, and a sense of accomplishment when the goals are achieved. Without goals, any Project will flounder, as there is nothing pushing it forward. Think of a journey with no destination and you see the problem. Goals should be as specific as possible in order to improve the chances of achieving the goals. It's the difference between driving to the Rockies, and driving to Denver.

Strategic objectives and goals associated with a DFSS Project naturally depend on exactly what kind of product or process we are trying to create. Typically, goal statements include:

- The Project's schedule, including the product's launch date

- The required level of quality, which can be defined by the product's durability, reliability, and appearance, for example; or a process's speed, accuracy, and consistency

- The costs incurred by the tasks and activities required, although a more detailed financial analysis will be listed in the Project budget

Similar lists of objectives would apply when the Project is focused on upgrading an existing product or process, or preparing to introduce it to new markets—though the lists usually function on a smaller scale.

DFSS Project Scope. This brings us to the Project Scope section of the charter, which serves to define just how big the Project will be and what it will cover. Think of it as outlining the field in which you'll be playing with chalk. This exercise won't tell you exactly what's going to happen between the lines once play begins, but it will tell you the confines of where the game will be played. And that in itself is very useful in making plans for what you want to do inside that area.

It's important to understand that some of the issues covered in the Project Scope are preliminary and subject to revision after the group completes more research in the following phases. Still, it's helpful to have a working model for the Project from the outset to give everyone involved some rough parameters of what to expect. That's why the scope questions are not set in stone, and should be treated as starting points. The scope needs to be easily revised or augmented as needed.

Think of it as a game of "hotter, colder" and you get the idea. Almost no one hits the bull's-eye on the first try, nor should they be expected to. But it's still helpful to make an estimate from which you can adjust up or down as needed, until you get hot hot hot.

An easy way to get the process started is to review already existing documents used for other Project kickoffs, and use them as a template for what you want to do now.

Here are a few questions that you might use to help define the scope of your Project:

- What customers are we targeting?

- What needs, internal or external, must we provide for?

- How much functionality is needed?

- What are the expected margins (profit, error, etc)?

- What are the anticipated volumes?

- When does the product or process need to be on the market?

- Does the scope include the whole system or a subsystem within a large system?

- Is the scope too big for one DFSS Project?

- Is the scope too small?

- What is the technical difficulty to achieve the target? It should be just right to challenge.

DFSS Project milestones. These are also vital to the success of the Project, and important to establish in the first phase of the DFSS Project. You can think of these milestones as subgoals for the Project, breaking down what can be a seemingly mammoth undertaking into smaller, more easily digestible bites.

While establishing milestones on Six Sigma Projects is important, it's even more important on DFSS Projects because the amount of innovation and information created between milestones is greater, the number of major events along the way is larger, and schedules tend to be longer. Where Six Sigma Projects are intended to fix existing products and processes, DFSS Projects are intended to reinvent the entire thing, and so they will necessarily take longer. Thus, to keep morale and momentum up and the Project focused over the long haul, it's very helpful to create shorter-term milestones. The milestones also serve to keep the Project on track along the way.

Sprinters don't need to break down each race into smaller segments, because the race is too short for that. But any marathon runner will tell you if you want to win a 26-mile race, you have to break it down into smaller segments, with different goals for each one. Complete each minirace correctly, and the marathon will take care of itself.

You can break down your "marathon" Project into the following miniraces with achievable goals:

- Lay out all key deliverables.

- Identify dates for accomplishment.

- Display on a time line.

- Communicate to all those who are supporting the activity.

- Get approval from the Sponsor and Champion.

The DFSS Project milestones can be integrated into the product development process milestones, or treated as separate deliverables or reviews. If they are treated as separate deliverables or reviews, then it is critical to get input from all of the key support areas involved. The reason for doing so is simple: it is not wise to assume that what you need from others will be available and ready when you want it. As they say, a failure to plan on your part does not constitute an emergency on their part. And don't forget this: You need their help a lot more than they need yours. The earlier you include them in your plans, the more likely it is you'll get their complete cooperation and support.

Milestones should be communicated in the simplest, most straightforward method possible. The clearer the recipe, the more likely the cake is going to come out right. One such method for doing so is by using the milestone chart, as shown in Figure 4.2.

You will notice that each milestone addresses only one key aspect of the overall charter. The purposes of the milestone chart are to break each goal down into even smaller goals, spread out the work, synchronize everyone's efforts, and facilitate tracking the Project.

The importance of estimating DFSS Project costs. The total cost for bringing a new product or process to market can be broken down into categories—such as product-related costs and nonproduct-related costs—and then broken down even further, the more specific, the better.

While getting a grip on the total cost is obviously important, in a DFSS Project you are primarily concerned with the cost and benefits associated with employing the tools and methods

---

FIGURE 4.2 | DFSS PHASE I/PART 1: MILESTONES

Week	0	1	2	3	4	5
Define Objectives		X				
Define Scope		X				
Establish Business Case		X				
Determine Budget			X			
Establish Milestones					X	
Start QFD						X

of DFSS. By separating out only those costs and revenues that DFSS created, you can hold DFSS accountable—something Total Quality Management did not dare do—and not allow those figures to hide in the hodgepodge of a division's total finances. The concept is analogous to keeping each individual player's scoring output—not just the team's—to see who's helping and who isn't.

By breaking down Project costs into smaller components you can track direct costs like labor, materials (that are used in the product), and facilities and equipment necessary to create the product or process, in addition to indirect costs such as overhead. These costs aren't hard to comprehend, of course, but they are often very hard for a company to accurately record.

The concept is a familiar one, based on an old but popular method of cost accounting, in which companies need to have an Activity Based Costing/Accounting (ABC) approach in order to estimate their system costs. If your company is already using ABC, this idea will be fairly straightforward.

To determine product- or process-related costs, first calculate:

- Variable costs

- Investment costs, such as facilities and tooling, launch, and engineering

The sum of these costs constitutes the total Project cost. From this amount, subtract nonproduct or nonprocess costs to determine the costs related to the product or process.

Quantify the DFSS Project benefits. Quantifying the benefits of a DFSS Project is not easy, but like anything else, practice makes perfect. The first time through is likely to result in errors, but by tracking the sources of these errors, you will begin to understand better how the numbers add up, and your estimates will improve. (When in doubt, consult a financial manager at your company.)

Profit = Sales volume × (Price – UMC) – (Overhead cost + Development cost + Cost of quality)

In order to increase profit—the ultimate goal of any free enterprise—you need to do one or more of the following:

- *Increase sales volume.* This can be achieved by meeting and exceeding the Voice of the Customer (VOC) or by reducing the price by reducing UMC and other costs.

- *Increase price.* This can be achieved by meeting and exceeding VOC.

- *Decrease UMC.* This can be achieved by developing an inexpensive concept, by optimizing product function, and/or by optimizing manufacturing process function.

- *Decrease overhead.* A transactional DFSS Project often achieves a reduction of overhead cost.

- *Decrease development cost including capital investment.* QFD and optimization will reduce this cost tremendously.

- *Decrease cost of quality.* A robust product or process will avoid typical costs of quality such as warranty, inspections, cost of process control, etc.

DFSS can contribute to one or, more often, many of the above simultaneously.

The benefits of first-pass estimates can include anticipated profit margin increases achieved through the increase in market price due to producing a better product or process; or expected cost reductions in variable cost of a product or process, development, verification, or manufacturing—in other words, being able to sell it at a higher price or deliver it at a lower cost.

Profits can also be improved through volume increases or cost reductions in after-sales support because making a better product or process will generate fewer complaints.

To summarize: Benefits can be drawn from efficiency improvements, such as:

- Reductions in cost of product or process

- Reductions in development cost

- Faster time to market

Benefits can also come from quality improvements, such as:

- Increasing market share through customer satisfaction

- Increased product or process (service) price

- Reduced costs for warranty and service

The DFSS Project budget. This can be integrated into the standard product or process development budget, or treated as a stand-alone item. If you decide to treat it as a separate item or document, it should contain only those deviations from the traditional product development—in other words, only the increase or decrease in costs compared to the previous business-as-usual costs for the same product or process.

For example, the expected cost for generating customer requirements for a given product or process will likely go up for a DFSS Project compared to a conventional product or process, because the Voice of the Customer is much more carefully gathered, analyzed, and heeded in DFSS Projects. But the costs for fixing quality and buying new equipment should go down because the results of a well-executed DFSS Project should have little need for debugging after the fact.

The team needs to ensure that costs for key additional resources are also included, and should note that those resources need to be scheduled or allotted for the Project. When it's time to create a more detailed budget, it is a must to get the accounting department involved when estimating cost and benefits.

DFSS is a proven methodology but it does require proper resources so that Project teams can fully execute and maximize benefits for the organization. The old saying "You can't expect the horse to run without letting it eat hay" makes the point. DFSS teams must determine the following:

- The incremental costs to deliver a DFSS product, which can be formatted to show cost per month

- Resources to be identified

- What team members may need to negotiate for people and facilities

Creating the DFSS Project Business Case

Your DFSS team begins creating the DFSS business case by estimating the expected return on investment (ROI). This is calculated by estimating project costs, anticipated volumes, and associated margins. The team also needs to take into account the company's required rate of return and its assumed net present value rate.

Other questions that need to be considered in the business case include:

- How would this Project affect our competitive position?

- How does it fit into our long-term strategy?

In a nutshell, the DFSS Project business case should answer the following questions:

- How does this Project fit with the strategic and financial objectives of the organization?

- Why is this Project worth doing?

- Why is it important to do it now?

- What are the consequences of NOT doing it?

The Project Plan

This will vary in size and complexity based on the size and complexity of the Project itself. The Project plan could be contained in a notebook or an electronic file. It is very important that the Black Belt develops a solid and respectable Project plan for the following reasons:

- Ideas that aren't written down float away. Putting them in writing makes them real.

- Things that are written down happen, things that are merely discussed do not.

- If you don't write it down, you'll have to explain it anew each time someone asks—or worse, be at the mercy of someone else explaining it for you.

- If you write it down, your Project plan can speak for you when you're not present—and circulate much more rapidly around the office.

- Things that are written down are taken seriously. Discussions are not. It's the difference between making a speech and writing a book. The book lasts, the speech doesn't.

To create a strong Project plan, you should address these key topics:

- Project charter

- Work Breakdown Structure (WBS)

- Detailed schedule

- Detailed budget

- Project staffing and resource requirements

- Progress reporting and change control

The information provided may change as the Black Belt learns more about the Project. For example, when the Black Belt initially prepares a Project plan, it will include only gross estimates of the schedule and budget. But as the schedule and budget come into sharper focus, the Project plan should be revised.

As a happy by-product, a good Project plan provides an excellent mechanism for collecting Project documentation so that the Project can be reviewed later on to learn the lessons necessary to improve and prepare for the next Project. Taking this one step further, the lessons learned need to be incorporated into the company's internal DFSS training material as *internal* Master Black Belts start training other Black Belts, after the *external* MBBs phase out. These lessons learned are highly valuable, paid for, and often not shared in other companies' case studies.

DFSS PHASE I/PART 2 (DEFINE) OVERVIEW

In DFSS Phase I/Part 2, you will:

- Identify methods of obtaining customer needs and wants.

- Obtain customer needs and wants, then organize them to list the Voice of Customer (VOC).

- Translate the Voice of the Customer into verifiable requirements.

The second part of Phase I deals with clearly defining the requirements of the product. The primary method to accomplish this is Quality Function Deployment, or QFD. The results of the

QFD process provide critical information and directions for the upcoming phases. Also included in Phase I/Part 2 are a variety of methods for gathering customer needs and turning them into solid requirement sets—basically, turning fuzzy customer desires into concrete product or process specifications.

The smartest businesspeople don't decide for themselves what the requirements of the product or process should be. They ask the customer and then work backwards. But to do this well, we first have to be able to distinguish between customer needs and customer complaints. It's the difference between before and after, of planning to please a customer and rushing to quiet them down.

A central theme for all DFSS Projects is the need to spend less time correcting mistakes and extolling the company fire fighters who do so, and more time preparing to avoid them and celebrating the less spectacular but more valuable planner. Distinguishing between customer complaints and needs is a great way to achieve this. The best way to eliminate customer complaints is to focus on their needs and deliver a product or process that not only meets them but also eliminates all the usual bugs that can ruin an otherwise good product or process. Thus, if the customer needs are going to be our guide, our next step is to define exactly who the customer is.

Who Is the Customer?

In general, the customer is the recipient of the product or process. More specifically, there are two types of customers:

1. External customers, or those who pay the bills or use the product or service

2. Internal customers, or those who help create the product or process

In DFSS, we are clearly focused on satisfying the external customers. But if we are too short-sighted, we will fail to see the vital role the internal customer plays in our attempt to please the external customer. Remember, the next processes all concern customers. So if you are designing a product, then it follows that the manufacturers, suppliers, salespeople, end users, and service and recycling personnel are *all* customers.

As a rule, American companies don't pay enough attention to their internal customers, and, almost no employees are able to be nice to the customer after being mistreated by their coworkers or bosses. A good rule of thumb: Treat your coworkers and employees as you'd have them treat your customers. What comes around goes around. Plan on it.

Let's start by studying the external customer, then apply this knowledge to help define the internal customer.

External customers. Some basic truths about customers include:

- Customers are people who purchase, use, handle, or regulate the product or service.

- You must obtain their voice, one way or another. Don't tell them what they want, ask them. Customers are individuals with a name, phone number, and address.

- It is easier, more pleasurable, and more profitable to focus on customer needs than customer complaints. Consider these three types of needs: Basic, Performance, and Excitement.

A truism of American business: We spend too much time on offense—discovering new and exciting ways to attract new customers, including billions on ad campaigns—and not enough on defense—coming up with better ideas to keep the customers we already have, including dull but effective strategies such as making better products, providing better service, and giving customers a say in how we serve them.

What is the current repurchase rate for your product? What could be done to improve the repurchase rate, aside from just lowering the price? What would it be worth to increase the repurchase rate by 10 percent?

Companies that have researched these questions have come up with the following discoveries:

- An insurance company determined that decreasing customer defections by just 5 percent increased its profits by 25 percent.

- A large manufacturing company estimated that a mere 1 percent increase in its customer repurchase rate, from 50 percent to 51 percent, produced an extra $100,000,000 in profits.

Generating and maintaining customers are both crucial if the company intends to stay in business and be profitable.

The basic concept of understanding customer needs is fairly simple, of course, but actually soliciting, quantifying, and applying customer needs to the design of a product or process takes a little more effort. It's the difference between knowing that your computer needs fixing and actually being able to fix it.

What you need is a formal, detailed methodology that teams can follow. This methodology will show you how to:

- Discover and decode what customers really need and want for today's and tomorrow's product or service and organize the Voice of the Customer.

- Convert VOC into actionable technical requirements, i.e., target and specification limits.

- Prioritize the requirements based on the strength of VOC, where you are relative to the best-in-class, and technical difficulty to achieve the target.

- Make intelligent decisions in the later phases of DFSS.

Understanding Customer Needs

More specifically, the process looks like this:

- Gather Voice of the Customer (VOC) input.

- Translate VOC into technical terms and prioritize.

- Establish requirements for the product or service based on prioritized VOC.

Next question: How do we capture customer needs and expectations, and translate those into actionable design requirements? Quality Function Deployment is the best approach for linking the objectives of inbound marketing with the requirements of engineering—in other words, converting customer wishes into specific corporate goals so that product/process designers know the right things to do. As a QFD practitioner put it in the mid-1980s: QFD should stand for "Quit Fooling with the Design, listen to our customers!"

Voice of the Customer is the cornerstone of developing any winning product or service, and how to gather the VOC is one of the biggest differences between QFD and traditional practices.

Traditionally, companies utilize marketing and customer service functions to obtain customer information—their wants and don't wants (complaints). While this information is important, it does not address the whole picture. Based on the Kano Model in QFD, there is a lot more than what the customers are saying. The Kano Model was developed by Dr. Kano in Japan while he was researching customer requirements for commercial airliners. As illustrated in Figure 4.3, the Kano Model represents an axes system where the horizontal axis represents the level of a company's fulfillment regarding a given customer want—not fulfilled at all on the left side to fulfilled completely on the right side—and the vertical axis represents the degree of customer satisfaction—very satisfied on the top to very dissatisfied at the bottom.

Let's look at an example. Suppose you're planning a Hawaiian vacation for the family and you call the hotel to make arrangements. Typically, questions you'd ask include: Are rooms available for the dates I'm looking at? Do you have rooms with an ocean view? Do you provide an airport shuttle service? Do you have an exercise facility? What is the room rate? Suppose the hotel staff on the phone tells you that the hotel can meet all your requirements (nonsmoking preference, ocean view room, free airport shuttle, etc.) and the room rate is $499 a night. You

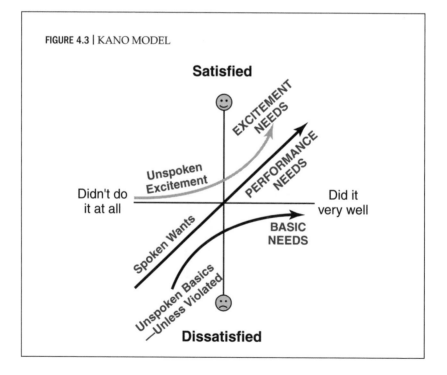

FIGURE 4.3 | KANO MODEL

the customer want a LOW room rate and their rate is HIGH; they didn't fulfill your need at all and you're very dissatisfied—you're in the lower left corner in the Kano Model. But suppose the hotel staff tells you that you can have all your preferences for $19.99 a night. You'd be extremely delighted—you're now in the upper right corner in the Kano Model. A customer requirement such as low room rate is a performance need in the Kano Model, a conscious purchase decision criterion.

Because the room rate is so reasonable, you book the room for a whole week and take your family there. As you get into your hotel room and start unpacking, one of your kids comes out of the bathroom and says: "There is no toilet paper in the bathroom!" How would you feel? Having toilet paper in the bathroom is something you wouldn't have asked for but if you don't have it, you'd be extremely dissatisfied. Right now, you're at the lower left corner in the Kano Model. On the other hand, suppose your kid comes out of the bathroom and says: "There are six rolls of toilet paper in the bathroom." Would you jump up and down and tell your spouse, "We've just found the perfect souvenir for your mother"? Having toilet paper in the bathroom is a basic need that goes unnoticed unless violated.

Now, suppose you check into your hotel room and find an umbrella hanging inside the closet with a note that reads: We at the XYZ hotel are trying to think of everything to make your stay pleasant. How would you feel? The last hotel you stayed at didn't provide an umbrella and you most likely weren't even aware of such an option so you felt nothing and were at the left center part in the Kano Model. But once you discover the umbrella in your room, the hotel provided very well and you're very satisfied—you're now at the upper right corner in the Kano Model. You've experienced the excitement need.

The point is this: Basic needs and excitement needs are usually unspoken and therefore, if you only do what the customers tell you to do—the performance need—you're providing only one-third of the equation.

The three types of customer needs in the Kano Model bear different impacts on the company in regard to the market position. Basic needs merely get the company into the market: "We can play the game because we have the basics." Performance needs well executed will only keep the company in the market, but providing the excitement needs well will gain the company the leadership position in the marketplace. The excitement needs are also called "customer delighters."

In DFSS, specific strategies are introduced to help companies define the spoken and unspoken customer needs, especially for excitement needs that typically represent future and unknown needs. Some examples of strategies include:

- *Customer modifications.* If the customers modify our products/services, there is obviously a need that has not been fulfilled. Uncover, develop, and include these modifications in our next generation product/service and generate customer excitement.

- *Lateral Benchmarking.* Companies can benchmark similar, but noncompeting products/services to borrow ideas. For example, automotive seat engineers can lateral benchmark airline seats and office furniture to help create the next generation of innovative products.

DFSS Quality Function Deployment (QFD)

QFD is a method used to translate the subjective wants and needs of the customer (VOC) into objective, quantifiable design requirements that can be used in designing better products or processes. QFD uses customer clinics, focus groups, surveys, and many other techniques to define and prioritize the customer wants and needs.

The traditional view of QFD shows the common flow of information and the linkages with those who need and use it. Figure 4.4 illustrates the four phases of QFD.

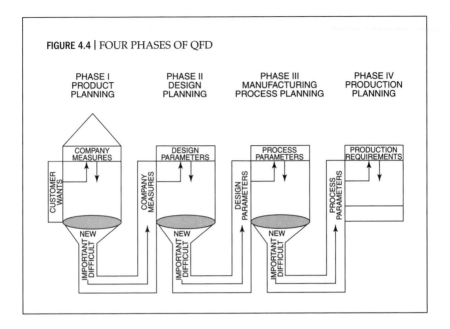

FIGURE 4.4 | FOUR PHASES OF QFD

This can also be absorbed sequentially, in the following seven-step process:

1. Understand who the customers are.

2. Capture and analyze the Voice of the Customer.

3. Translate the Voice of the Customer into performance requirements.

4. Choose the best design concept to meet the performance requirements.

5. Translate the performance requirements into product/ service design parameters.

6. Translate the product parameters into manufacturing conditions (this step does not apply to a service).

7. Determine activities required to maintain manufacturing conditions or service process parameters.

In DFSS-QFD, however, we're able to address Steps 4, 5, 6, and 7 by employing several other tools to get the jobs done—namely, TRIZ, the Pugh Concept Selection Technique, Robust Design®, and Process Control methods. (All these are discussed in greater detail in Chapters 5, 6, and 7.)

The DFSS-QFD process provides greater objectivity, greater focus, and greater speed than the more traditional process of understanding customer needs. DFSS-QFD also produces a prioritized list of customer wants. DFSS-QFD intertwines customer and competitive information to help shape the design requirements.

The DFSS-QFD process requires Project designers to adopt a greater customer focus—the foundation of DFSS. Doing business the old way, a team would select a product or process design, then draw up specifications for that design—all on the assumption that meeting those specifications will create customer satisfaction, WITHOUT truly knowing what the customer wants are. Even worse, sometimes teams would proceed WITHOUT truly understanding the customer base, therefore missing the wants and needs of some customers.

This is tantamount to a chef deciding to make chicken à la king and sending it to the customer's table without knowing what the customer wants to eat.

With DFSS-QFD, however, the process is reversed and refined. Instead of telling the customers what they want, the chef ASKS them what they want, breaks down the responses to the finest possible details—How do they want the meal prepared? Soup or salad? Dressing? With garlic or without?—and then goes about the process of meeting those specifications before returning to the customer's table with the final product.

In DFSS-QFD, the specifications for customer acceptance are written prior to selecting the design. This requires the team to understand more fully and deeply who all the customers are and what their needs and expectations are BEFORE deciding on a design concept. This is why some practitioners have also named DFSS-QFD the "customer driven product/service development."

An office equipment company in New England practiced DFSS-QFD extensively, achieved tremendous gains, and even took this to the next level. They printed on the cover of the company product brochure: Customer Designed Products.

One tool used to help accomplish this is the DFSS-QFD House of Quality (see Figure 4.5).

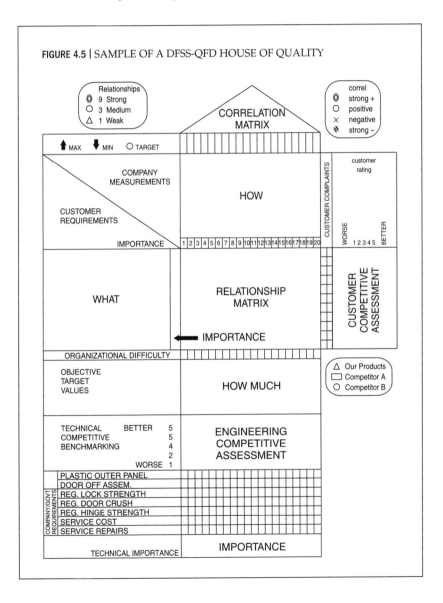

FIGURE 4.5 | SAMPLE OF A DFSS-QFD HOUSE OF QUALITY

As you can see, the DFSS-QFD process consists of linked information arranged along the horizontal, customer-focused axis, and an intersecting vertical, internally focused technical axis.

In this case, the horizontal axis addresses only external customers. The items on that axis help identify, quantify, and prioritize customer needs and desires. The vertical axis contains internal performance specifications and other crucial elements that will help the DFSS team achieve customer wants and needs.

One of these crucial elements is the intersection of these axes, the relationship matrix. It identifies how well the internal performance specifications can satisfy the customer's needs and desires.

The DFSS-QFD customer axis includes:

- Customer needs and wants

- Customer importance ratings

- Customer competitive evaluations

- Subjective customer targets

Those are the basics. Here are the specifics. The customer axis answers the following questions:

- What do our existing and potential customers want?

- Which of those desires are highly important to the customers?

- How good do we have to be to achieve customer satisfaction?

- How do our customers perceive how well we've satisfied those desires compared to our competition?

- In what areas are we trailing behind our competition and really need to catch up?

- If we can't achieve everything the customers want, what are our priorities based on the customer importance ratings and customer competitive evaluations?

- Are there opportunities where no provider is satisfying the customers and if we excel in these areas, can we drastically increase market share?

- What other opportunities do we have to get an even bigger advantage over the competition?

Now, the DFSS-QFD technical axis includes:

- Correlation matrix

- Performance measures

- Relationship matrix

- Degrees of difficulties (in achieving targets)

- Technical competitive benchmarking

- Technical targets and specifications to beat the toughest competitor

- Safety and regulatory requirements

- Technical importance ratings

The technical axis is designed to answer these questions:

- What technical specifications can directly impact customer satisfaction for one or more criteria? (In other words, can we hit more than one bird with each stone?)

- Which technical specifications are the most vital for achieving customer satisfaction (as defined by the customer, not us)?

- Are there conflicts between technical specifications that desperately need to be resolved?

- Is there anything missing in our technical specifications to indicate that we're not addressing ALL the customer wants? A blank row in the relationship matrix will reveal this.

- Do we have unnecessary technical specifications that will require development resources to achieve but will add no value to the customers? A blank column in the relationship matrix will pinpoint this.

- How do our current products and services compare to the competition when benchmarking using these technical criteria?

- What targets should we set for technical specifications in order to achieve the level of customer satisfaction defined in the customer axis?

- What regulatory requirements must be satisfied to sell products in the target market?

The results we get from the DFSS-QFD are used throughout the DFSS Project. They are the basic ingredients of the rich stew to follow. Just as the quality of the ingredients determines the quality of the meal to follow, the data we gather and use in Phase I is vital to the quality of our solutions later in the DFSS process.

In DFSS Phase II, for example, we will use this data to identify superior design concepts in conjunction with the TRIZ methodology, which will be explained later. Likewise, the prioritized requirements will clearly direct our choice of design concept when combined with the Pugh Concept Selection Technique. Selected concepts will be optimized for nominal values and tolerances through Robust Design techniques.

Each potential concept will be assessed for potential problems BEFORE it is rolled out. The tool of choice here is the Failure Mode and Effects Analysis (FMEA), which is explained in detail in Chapter 5. DFSS-QFD will provide many critical inputs to the FMEA process.

DFSS-QFD will also provide the starting point for defining the Ideal Function that we will use in Robust Design to optimize our system specifics. Prioritized performance measures will be carried through the DFSS process and ultimately drive our logic for establishing which product parameters and respective process conditions require special controls.

DFSS-QFD links. The work done in DFSS-QFD will benefit later phases.

- The outputs are used to select better design concepts (DFSS Phase II).

- Performance measures, Voice of the Customer, and environmental context are used to drive the Failure Mode and Effects Analysis (DFSS Phase II).

- The design will be optimized using the Ideal Function approach to meet multiple, if not all, performance measures (DFSS Phase III).

- CTQ design parameters and targets deployed from DFSS Phase III guide the implementation of manufacturing and service processes, the development of control plans needed to sustain the quality and performance delivered to customers (DFSS Phase IV).

When Phase I is complete, the stage is set to mobilize the information, organization, and commitment in the first phase to begin to look for solutions in Phase II.

C H A P T E R   5

Develop
Concepts

The key deliverables from DFSS Phase I are the prioritized customer requirements and targets. These requirements and targets will focus the DFSS team efforts as we proceed to Phase II. Because we now know what the right things to do are, we must next ask ourselves:

- Do we have a product or service concept in mind?

- Does our concept even have a chance to achieve the customer requirements and targets?

- If the answer is no to either of the first two questions, how do we come up with a concept that does have a chance?

- If we have several concepts to choose from, which one has the best chance?

- How do we make sure our selected concept, if deployed, will have minimal risk?

In DFSS Phase II, proven tools and methods are used to answer these questions, including TRIZ (the theory for inventive problem solving), Pugh (a technique for evaluating and developing concepts), and FMEA (the Failure Mode and Effects Analysis, which manages risks to mitigate failures).

A maxim for investigative journalists is: Follow the money. Our guiding principle for Phase II will be: Follow the deliverables. The most important deliverable from Phase II is a concept that not only has the best chance to meet customer requirements, but is also free of failure potential.

Our objectives for Phase II are therefore to:

- Identify viable concepts through creative methods.

- Use logical, objective methods to evaluate alternatives.

- Identify and eliminate potential product/service failures.

Basically, this means we'll need creative techniques to come up with alternative concept solutions, then test those alternatives with reliable, objective analytical methods and perform a risk analysis to ensure that the alternative chosen is free of serious failure potential.

IDENTIFY CONCEPTS

The first objective of Phase II is to identify concepts. There are several effective means to generate ideas including brainstorming, a related process called brainwriting, assumption busting, and TRIZ. We will cover the first three that are fairly popular, familiar approaches, then dive in more deeply with the TRIZ method, which is probably the least well known of the group, but the most important to DFSS.

Brainstorming is a well-known but commonly misapplied method for generating a lot of ideas quickly. The basic notion, as you probably know, is to get a few people sitting around a table, pick a question, and create as many ideas for solving it as possible.

I'll discuss some variations on the basic approach shortly, but in all cases a few guidelines need to be understood.

There are no bad ideas in brainstorming. The goal is to open up the creative floodgates and let it all come out. This is how you get past the obvious, "safe" ideas and discover the bolder, more innovative gems.

If you were coaching a basketball team, you wouldn't put a player into the game, say good luck, and then add, "Oh, by the way, one missed shot and you're out!" The kid wouldn't have a chance. He'd be bound to miss his first shot. So when you launch this exercise, the rule is: This is not *Family Feud* and you're not out after three strikes. ANY answer is a good "answer."

The most important goal in brainstorming is QUANTITY, not QUALITY. Don't worry. You'll be surprised how many good answers you get! You'll also be surprised how often a silly idea generates three or four good ones following it. Team members need to keep this in mind: Don't criticize crazy ideas, IMPROVE them!

Set a goal for the total number of ideas. Thirty ideas is a fair target. It may seem impossible at first, but once people get going, they'll easily surpass it. The high goal also encourages them to work fast and not "think" too much. Again, ANY idea is a good one—doesn't matter if it's silly, a copy-cat, or impractical. Just let the wheels turn!

It's even better if you have more than one team and create a little competition among friends. This ensures fast movement!

Set a time limit. The shorter the better. Three minutes, be-lieve it or not, is fair—plenty of time for a focused team to gen-erate 30 ideas (50–60 is not uncommon). Like preparing your tax returns, if you had no deadline, it'd take forever. This forces the team to MOVE—and in so doing, they remove many of the blocks to generating creative solutions. It actually helps, not hurts.

Give them a problem to solve, right before beginning.
Make it clear and direct. To keep things loose and show how the process works, you might consider giving them a sample subject first, like coming up with possible uses for a rake handle. (You can use it as a stake for tomatoes in the garden, a "lock" for a sliding glass door, a limbo stick, a baseball bat—and even a rake handle!)

When they're done with the sample and they see how effectively brainstorming works, they'll be sold on it and ready to try the real thing. Give them the problem you're trying to solve, be it fixing a persistent jamming area in a photocopier or solving the morning rush at a car dealership service department. Then let it fly!

Create a slightly chaotic, energetic atmosphere. "Ready, set, go!" Move around the room making sure they're all on task and giving a jump start where needed. Be a little manic about yelling out the time. Move, move, move!

Use the "say it, write it, toss it" technique to record ideas.
The traditional approach of "one recording secretary jotting down ideas" has a major problem: the team can only move as quickly as the secretary can understand and write. Instead, have each team member:

- Say the idea out loud so that everyone else hears.

- Write down his/her idea on a sticky note.

- Toss the written note to the middle of the table.

This approach alleviates the recording secretary's time bottleneck and is one of the best ways to generate a lot of ideas in a short time because most people don't want to have fewer ideas than the other team members in the spirit of friendly competition.

After they're finished, have them total the number of responses. They'll be amazed! Not just 30, but 40 or 50. Then tell them, "Okay, that's a lot. But how many of these ideas do you think are impractical or just plain silly?" Their estimates will run way over 50 percent, usually up to 70 or 80 percent. Now ask them to circle the clearly impractical responses and total them up to create a percentage of the total. They'll be stunned again to discover that only 10 to 20 percent of their answers aren't workable, and that they came up with over two dozen viable solutions—in just three minutes!

Just for fun, ask them how their silly ideas occurred. If they're like most groups, they'll find that they came up with an impractical notion about every four or five answers followed by a flurry of good ones. When they stalled again, someone said something funny and got the ball rolling once more.

As the Jesuits say, "Freedom within Discipline." Or, as General Patton liked to say, "Don't tell them how to get there. Just tell them where they need to end up, and they'll find many more creative ways of getting there than you could ever think of."

And THAT is how you manage creativity!

Now, within the "brainstorming family," there are a few variations you can use to better fit whatever issue you're grappling with. These modified brainstorming techniques include: channel, analogy, anti-solution, brainwriting, and assumption busting.

Channel brainstorming requires team members to focus on a subcategory of the issue in question to make a large task a lot more manageable.

Analogy brainstorming allows participants to focus on a parallel issue, as analogies do, to avoid tension that might be associated with more controversial topics, while still generating answers that could be helpful to resolve the real dilemma. After the brainstorming session, participants will then link their answers to the "unspoken" issue, and be happily surprised to discover they might just have untied the knot.

Anti-solution brainstorming asks team members to go in the exact opposite direction by coming up with ideas to make the product or process *worse,* in much the same manner that a good attorney tries to punch holes in his own argument. By doing so, the team will discover ways to protect their work from failure and make the product or process much better—even foolproof. This can be a lot of fun, too.

Brainwriting is, simple enough, brainstorming in written form. Needless to say, less vocal people often prefer this method to the traditional one.

This is how it works: Each team member writes down an idea for the proposed concept or solution to a problem on a piece of paper or file card, and then passes it to the next team member, who adds to the idea, modifies it, or submits his or her own new idea. To be more ambitious about it, you should start with one piece of paper for each team member, and pass them all at the same time—not unlike a game of cards—which generates still more ideas.

The basic principles of brainstorming, however, must be intact. Specifically, the anything-goes philosophy must hold—which is harder to maintain when people are writing because most people consider writing more formal. And the initial goal should be simply generating a large quantity of ideas. No judging is the rule.

After a few rounds of this—you might still stick with a time limit, to add energy and decrease hesitation—you can call stop, add up the number of ideas, cross out the crazy ones, and start sifting through the most promising ideas. Give each member one of the answer sheets to review and begin the sorting process.

Often times a clear theme will emerge, with several of the ideas contributing to it. This can lead to an easier consensus than you might get with the other approaches. After all, when everyone has contributed to the solution, they're more likely to support it.

Assumption busting is exactly what it sounds like: questioning the status quo by thinking beyond what it is today or what might be possible tomorrow. As Robert F. Kennedy said, while many look at what is and ask "Why?," he looked at what could be and asked, "Why not?" That is just the kind of thinking assumption busting is designed to encourage.

Take temperature tolerances. While a company might believe that a certain product has to be stored at 39 degrees with a tolerance of plus or minus 2 degrees, partly because it's been the standard for years, a more questioning employee might discover upon testing that some products can tolerate plus or minus 5 degrees, while others must be tightened to plus or minus 1 degree. The adjusted tolerances will create lower costs in the first case, and higher quality and efficiency in the second.

Another example: the U.S. auto industry, which had been atop the world market for so long, barely knew how to respond when the Japanese and others started making higher-quality, better-selling vehicles in the 1980s. All too often, when asked why one policy or the other was still in place, the answer was, "Because we've been doing it this way for decades." The Japanese infusion forced the better executives to rethink this old response and question the way they had been doing business. From such reconsiderations came the revived Chrysler Corporation; the customer-friendly Saturn dealerships, which revolutionized the ways cars are sold; and the rise of the SUV and the minivan.

As you might imagine, newer and less experienced employees tend to work more naturally at assumption busting than experienced workers. Likewise, the technique is especially effective on mature products and processes that often have built-in and calcified constraints whose origins no one can remember.

Clearly, when you're sitting in a boat stuck in a frozen lake, it's time to break the ice. Assumption busting does just that.

Here are a few "rules" that have bitten the dust throughout history, busted by people who were not afraid to question built-in assumptions:

- The world is flat.

- The sun revolves around the earth.

- People cannot govern themselves.

- Electricity can never be harnessed.

- Man will never fly.

- Man will never walk on the moon.

- Computers will never be small enough for personal use.

- Packages cannot be delivered overnight.

Clinging to the old way of thinking stopped everyone else from creating these solutions, except Christopher Columbus, Copernicus, Thomas Jefferson, Benjamin Franklin, the Wright Brothers, Neil Armstrong, Steven Jobs, and Fred Smith, among others. That's why we remember their names, and not the names of the thousands of people who said it couldn't be done simply because it never happened.

Granted, all of these people paid a price for their revolutionary thinking, but in the end all were vindicated. It's important, therefore, to create the kind of environment on your DFSS team that does not punish creativity, but rewards it. The first step toward doing so is never judging "bad" ideas. You need not act on every idea, of course, but never scold anyone for coming up with potential solutions, no matter how far-fetched the ideas may be.

INTRODUCTION TO TRIZ

The reasons designers (those who engineer both products or processes) can develop blind spots to innovation are many. They are under immense pressure to be innovative while working under increasingly short development time restrictions on products and processes that have grown dauntingly complex, and have short life cycles.

But what was considered excellent yesterday is merely average today. Overnight delivery, faxes, and e-mail are now ho-hum facts of daily life, not whiz-bang marvels. Customers have more choices for virtually every purchase they make than at any time in human history, and they are accordingly more educated and selective about their purchases. Thus, the only answer for most companies is to be more creative than the competition.

In today's competitive marketplace, one of the few sustainable advantages a company can possess is innovation. The catch to innovation, though—unlike, say, cost-cutting or time-saving measures—is that it's unpredictable. Many people sing in the shower but how many actually jump out and scream "Eureka" because an innovative idea had just clicked?

Innovation can be made more manageable through TRIZ, or the Theory of Inventive Problem Solving, a structured approach to evolving systems. TRIZ was developed by Genrich Altshuller from patterns he analyzed when reviewing thousands of patent applications. From these, Altshuller developed a set of principles for cultivating inventions in order to eliminate corporate contradictions and problems.

Thinking he was on to something, Altshuller distilled the knowledge contained in over a million patents to provide the solutions needed for almost any product or process conflict. The source of this knowledge base is illustrated in Figure 5.1. Altshuller then developed 40 Inventive Principles from his findings, principles that can be applied to any field of design and create innovative solutions.

Systematic Innovation may seem an oxymoron, like jumbo shrimp, but with TRIZ, individuals can generate amazingly creative solutions without threatening the stability of the company—all in a step-by-step process that takes some of the fear and guesswork out of innovation.

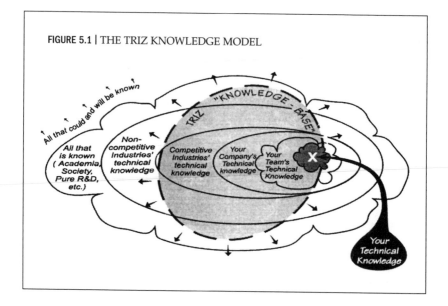

FIGURE 5.1 | THE TRIZ KNOWLEDGE MODEL

The reason DFSS-TRIZ works so effectively is the simple fact that over 90 percent of the underlying generic problems product and process designers face today at a given company have already been solved at another company or even in a completely different industry—perhaps even for entirely unrelated situations—using a fundamentally different technology or approach.

More specifically, TRIZ is founded on three premises:

1. The "ideal" design will produce the desired functions without the existence of the system.

2. Innovative designs resolve contradictions.

3. It is important to look at the past, present, and future of the system design.

The TRIZ process starts with a questionnaire, called the Innovative Situation Questionnaire (ISQ), which is designed to gather all of the information needed to analyze the problem under consideration. Once the real problem (conflict) is identified, it is converted from an industry-specific problem to a generic problem by stripping away the subject matter. In TRIZ, generic problems have generic solutions. The team will then explore the generic solution paths to eventually create an industry-specific solution.

For example, let's say we design and manufacture overhead projectors and the problem we face today is that the mechanical arm that holds the mirror and magnifying lens tends to crack, resulting in warranty issues. A well-known solution to the problem is increasing wall thickness of the mechanical arm but if we do so, the projector becomes too heavy. The industry-specific conflict is "mechanical arm cracking" versus "projector too heavy." If we strip away the subject matter, the generic problem becomes a "strength" versus "weight" conflict (by the way, there is often more than one way to define the generic problem, "reliability" versus "cost," for example). Most likely, someone else from some industry at some point in time MUST have solved this problem before. The TRIZ methodology contains generic solutions to the "strength" versus "weight" conflict, including:

- *Segmentation.* Instead of making the product in one piece, how about making it with several smaller modules that need to be assembled? Would that solve our problem? Does this give us any ideas?

- *Copying.* Instead of an unavailable, expensive, or fragile design, use simpler and inexpensive copies (e.g., conduct team meetings using videoconferencing, fax, e-mail, or a videophone instead of team members physically being together). Does this give us any ideas?

- *Inexpensive short-life.* Instead of making the product strong and light forever, can we use the "disposable" concept to make it strong and light for a shorter life? Would that work for us? Does this give us any ideas?

- *Composites.* Instead of using homogeneous material, how about nonhomogeneous material? Does this give us any ideas?

Even with this simple example, a typical team will probably come up with more than 20 ideas easily, and that's only by exploring four of the many generic solution paths available. A team that thoroughly applies TRIZ to this problem can generate a lot more ideas, therefore increasing the probability of hitting on one that will really work, as opposed to another team that only has two ideas to choose from and needs to somehow make one work.

TRIZ does not give the team the detailed design solution, but it points the team to focused and clear directions for innovation. Traditional innovation methods can work only to the level of knowledge and experience of the people involved. But because the TRIZ methodology is based on technology, not psychology, even noncreative individuals can capitalize on the power of TRIZ and create innovations in no time.

EVALUATING CONCEPTS

Once many potential solutions are identified, the second goal in DFSS Phase II is to select the best solution to the problem at hand. To do this, the first step is to ferret out the impractical concepts from our long list of possibilities, then narrow the list to just a few of the most promising prospects (usually two or three). The team needs to flesh them out, combine ideas, determine what it would take to put them in motion, including conducting a cost-benefit analysis, then follow up with a risk-potential problem analysis. From there, it should be relatively easy to determine which solution concept to deploy for the next step, Phase III: optimize the design.

To explore these tasks in greater detail, let's address the first step: ferreting out the impractical solutions from our long list of possibilities. This is called screening for acceptable solutions.

This is accomplished by first eliminating those solutions that lack any of our nonnegotiable criteria, which could include legal requirements, safety issues, company policies, or customer-derived specifications. (Although it should be noted that if company policies alone are preventing the team from pursuing an otherwise stellar idea, that policy should be studied more closely for any possible wiggle room.)

The next step is to estimate a solution's likely benefit to the company, against the estimate of the likely cost of the solution. The point is, even if a solution works, it may not be worth doing if it requires a very long "run" for too short a "slide." Some other solutions should be investigated.

This is the triage method of management, something Americans too often don't grasp. The question is not "should we do this or not?" but "should we do this or find a better solution?" Just because a solution will provide marginal help to the company doesn't mean it's worth our time and effort. We want to get the maximum payoff for the minimum effort whenever we can. Look for the low-lying fruit first.

One way to determine which is the lowest-lying, juiciest fruit is to create a scatter diagram, in which each solution is plotted on a scale pitting effort and cost on one axis against benefits on the other. In this way, the overall "return on effort" of each solution can be readily compared.

Evaluation Methods

After the initial screening is done, there are three methods to pick the one solution the group will pursue:

1. Multi-Voting (also called the Nominal Group Technique)

2. Criteria-Based Matrix

3. Pugh Concept Selection Technique

Regardless of the specific method you choose, you might elect, as many do, to attack the selection process in two phases, by first performing an initial review to narrow the list to the top few choices—creating the proverbial short list—and then "war-gaming" the possible consequences of each individual choice, trying to determine their possible outcomes. Once that exercise is complete, making a final review of the remaining choices should produce a clear winner. At that point, you're ready to proceed.

Multi-Voting (also called Nominal Group Technique) helps teams narrow down the top three or four candidates *quickly*. The main advantages of this method are agreement and especially speed. It also should be a fun, energetic exercise.

Here's how it works: First, make a simple laundry list of all the concept candidates—possibly a dozen or two, thanks to our innovation session early on—on a flip chart or white board, then give each team members five Post-it notes to stick on their favorite ideas. They can choose to spread their votes out among five candidates or concentrate their voting power on one or two, as they see fit. Thus, strength of conviction counts. (This is why it's called Multi-Voting.)

As you might expect, the group should pursue the top three or four ideas, depending on where the drop-off point is in the voting. You don't want less than three ideas, or creativity and debate will be stifled in the next round, and more than five will make the next step be too time-consuming.

The *Criteria-Based Matrix* is more detailed and rigorous than the Multi-Voting method. The first step in this approach is to weight the selection criteria, NOT by asking the team members what they feel is important, but by consulting the Voice of the Customer as captured in the Quality Function Deployment. They, not us, must determine how each idea will be judged, which they can do through surveys, focus groups, and even buying patterns. This should be a relatively straightforward process, as it requires very little judgment on the part of the team members. Each criterion should be assigned a number on a 1-to-5 scale, with 5 being the most important in the customer's eyes.

The team members will be tested on the next step, when it's time to determine how well each concept candidate satisfies each customer-driven criterion. In this case, you can use a 1-to-5 or a 1-to-10 scale, the highest number being the best. After each team member gives each concept a score on each criterion, the team members' ratings are averaged for each item, then *multiplied* by the weighted number of each criterion. In other words, a concept's performance on a given customer specification is then multiplied by its previously determined level of importance— much the way an Olympic diver's score is derived by multiplying his or her performance by the dive's level of difficulty. Then, of course, as in the Olympics, the concept with the highest score wins.

The advantages of this are several, including detailed analysis, customer focus, and a more scientific approach to the conclusion. It may give team members (and other employees) greater confidence in the solution selected, and also make the team members feel it was less subjective. It is, however, usually more time-consuming and rigorous than the Multi-Voting method.

Stuart Pugh often used the Criteria-Based Matrix, but felt that it could be improved, so he developed the *Pugh Concept Selection Technique*, the preferred method of designing products with Six Sigma capabilities.

The Pugh Concept Selection Technique minimizes or eliminates many of the downsides of the Criteria-Based Matrix, because it is easier and faster. One reason is that it concerns itself only with the customers' most important criteria, thus dramatically reducing the number of permutations possible, and the time needed to examine such a large batch.

The Pugh method further reduces time by eliminating the 1-to-10 ranking of each concept on each criterion, replacing the time-consuming approach with a simple better (plus), worse (minus), or about the same (S, or 0) evaluation, relative to the current product (in the case where there is no current product, use any of the concept candidates as the baseline concept). Ratings are given as each new solution or concept is evaluated against the current or baseline concept, on a criterion-by-criterion basis, so the new solutions are not evaluated against each other.

In essence, this is equivalent to converting the highly detailed and occasionally confusing five-star method of movie ratings to the simple thumbs up/thumbs down approach of Roger Ebert. While it's not as exact, it usually does the trick.

After the team members have rated each concept on the customer's criteria with a plus, minus, or zero, the team leader totals the pluses, minuses, and zeros, and narrows down the competition to the three or four concepts with the most pluses and the fewest minuses. At this point, a powerful attribute of the Pugh method is invoked, namely, attacking the weaknesses and enhancing the strengths of the surviving alternatives. This synthesis process of using the strong points of weaker concepts to strengthen the weak aspects of stronger alternatives is in itself a significant creative process. The result of this synthesis process, called Controlled Convergence, is to create stronger concepts than any of the original alternatives.

Analyzing the Pugh Matrix often leads to new solutions by combining the best of several worlds. If there is one solution that is clearly the best, but there are still negatives for that solution in the matrix, there is still room for improvement. During the analysis phase of the matrix, a team member might find a new solution that utilizes most of the elements of the highest-score solution, but finds a way to remove negative aspects from that solution by combining aspects from one of the remaining solutions.

A confirmation run of the matrix can also be used to verify that the selected concept is indeed the best. To conduct the confirmation run, simply repeat the process but use the selected best solution as the baseline and compare all other solutions to it. This now allows for a one-on-one comparison of the selected solution against all proposed solutions. If it is indeed the best, the other solutions will have many more minuses than pluses.

Now, the $64,000 question: When should a team use which of these three methods? Here's a handy guide:

1. *Multi-Voting* is usually the most effective method when you need a quick way to reach consensus.
   Downside: Your conclusions are based solely on the subjective opinions of the team members.

2. *Criteria-Based Matrix* is best when you're seeking a more detailed, objective method for concept selection.
   Downside: It takes more time to do it well.

3. *Pugh Concept Selection Technique* combines the best of both worlds, provided your selection process does not have any overwhelming needs for either speed or detail. Further, the Controlled Convergence process goes beyond concept selection to synthesize improved concepts that are stronger than any of the original ideas.
   Downside: Criteria considered must be fairly equally important, because they are not weighted against each other.

Obviously, each method has its strengths and weaknesses. To sum this up, the Multi-Voting method is quick and fun, but is at the mercy of the subjective judgments of team members. If you and the rest of the company trust their judgment, it might be the way to go. The Criteria-Based Matrix greatly increases the objectivity of the process (and with it, possibly the credibility of the conclusions elsewhere in the company) but it also increases the time needed to complete it, and the potential for conflict. The Pugh method features the speed of Multi-Voting and the customer-driven focus of the Criteria-Based Matrix, but might not be the right choice if you are looking for a fast conclusion. However, it is the right choice if you are seeking the most creativity and rigor.

Which method to use, of course, is up to each team, and should be determined based on the team consensus.

Potential Problem Analysis

After the team has settled on one concept to pursue using any of the above methods, it will embark on the last step of DFSS Phase II: potential problem analysis. The idea behind this is simply to discover and eliminate potential bugs BEFORE money is spent pursuing the concept selected.

The basic four-step approach to doing so is very straightforward:

1. Identify the potential unintended consequences of the chosen concept.

2. Prioritize them based on both the odds of them occurring and the potential damage they could create.

3. Determine ways the concept design could be altered to avoid the highest-risk problems.

4. Implement the debugging plans.

No matter how great a concept might seem during the planning stages, if these pitfalls are not corrected, it will result in abject failure. Arguably the best way to accomplish the four tasks above is the aforementioned Failure Modes and Effects Analysis process, or FMEA. In a nutshell, it's a means to consider potential product failures, analyze the risks associated with those failures, and organize them in a useful way for taking action.

FAILURE MODES AND EFFECTS ANALYSIS

Created during the 1960s by the aerospace industry—a field that knows better than any other that failure is not an option—FMEA quickly transcended its original domain to become a dominant theory in the consumer markets as well. Not surprisingly, the first consumer product companies to adopt the FMEA strategy in the 1970s were those most vulnerable to liability lawsuits, such as automotive companies. These companies became quick converts to FMEA to reduce potential lawsuits by eliminating failure modes during the design phase, especially in terms of safety-related issues. In 1994, FMEA became formally required by QS-9000 for all automotive suppliers.

Since the 1970s, FMEA has expanded its reach to include customer satisfaction, in which FMEA is used to reduce not just customer lawsuits but customer complaints. This not only improves market share, but it's an even better way to avoid lawsuits, by nipping them in the bud when the stakes are much lower.

The first step in the FMEA process is to take a logical, unemotional approach to coming up with a list of any and all possible product or process failures, and determine the consequences of the failures. Figure 5.2 is a sample FMEA form that companies can use to record possible failures. Next, the group needs to assess the likelihood of failures occurring, and the ability to detect or prevent failures before the product reaches the customer. Naturally, it's the combination of severity of consequences, likelihood of failure occurrence, and detection ability that determines how seriously a threat to quality should be taken.

For example, if you're running a major league baseball team, the odds of it raining on at least one of your 81 home games is quite high. Because it will not happen very often, AND because the only downside it will create is costing you "rain checks" for the fans who attended that day, the risk probably doesn't

FIGURE 5.2 | FMEA FORM

Failure Modes and Effects Analysis (FMEA)										

Process or Product Name:					Prepared by:			Page __ of __		
Responsible:					FMEA Date (Orig) _____ (Rev) _____					

Process Step/Part Number	Potential Failure Mode	Potential Failure Effects	S E V	Potential Causes	O C C	Current Controls	D E T	R P N	Actions Recommended
What are the process steps?	In what ways can the process step go wrong?	What is the impact of the Failure Mode on the customer?	How severe is the effect on the customer?	What are the causes of the Failure Mode?	How often can the Cause or Failure Mode occur?	What are the existing controls and procedures that prevent the Cause or Failure Mode?	How well can you detect the Cause or Failure Mode?	Calculated	What are the actions for reducing the occurrence, decreasing severity or improving detection?
								0	
								0	
								0	
								0	
								0	
								0	
								0	
								0	
								0	
								0	
								0	

warrant taking extraordinary preventive measures like building a domed roof over the ballpark—especially when doing so can ruin the ambiance of the game, thus turning away customers.

However, the chances of a pitched ball being fouled off into the stands directly behind home plate, at 90 miles per hour, is very high. It will occur several times every game (occurrence), even the most athletic fans may not be able to react fast enough (detect), and the potential damage done could include severe injuries and even death to fans (severity). This clearly needs to be addressed in a fail-safe manner. And that's why every major league team has spent thousands installing elaborate netting behind home plate, but only a handful play inside domed ballparks.

The information gained in these first steps of the FMEA process drive the prioritization process. The next step is taking the actions necessary to reduce or eliminate the higher risk issues, for example, installing the foul ball netting.

When completing the FMEA process, it's important to have input from a number of different sources and divisions of the company. The more creative you can be about the potential problems your concept might incur, the more likely you can plan for and squelch them before rolling it out. The key here is to find as many devil's advocates as you can. The wider DFSS core team, for example, often makes an excellent sounding board for this stage, while specialists in a variety of subjects will invariably think of problems you probably could not have come up with yourself. This is just like proofreading—it's easier for someone else to point out the mistakes in your writing.

The DFSS core team consists of the design engineer, the manufacturing (or process) engineer, suppliers, and the test engineers, while the support team roster includes the quality engineer, the service engineer, legal counsel, specialists from purchasing or accounting, and the system or next process engineer.

ALL should be consulted about possible design pitfalls before proceeding. Not only will this result in a far more comprehensive list of problems—and how to solve them—but it will greatly increase the cooperation and credibility you enjoy across the company. It's also an insurance policy against the inevitable conclusion whenever a product or process fails: "Well, no one ever asked me." So *ask them.*

The six objectives of the DFSS-FMEA process are:

1. Identify potential failures.

2. Rate them by severity of failure consequences.

3. Rank them by likelihood of occurrence.

4. Estimate your ability to detect or prevent failures.

5. Identify critical-to-quality (CTQ) characteristics.

6. Focus on eliminating or preventing the most serious problems from occurring.

All six of these objectives can be packaged as deliverables to the DFSS team, including the CTQs which are derived from the cause-and-effect relationship of errors on product or process quality, especially on those items the customers deem most important to their satisfaction. Product CTQs will often warrant installing special controls during the manufacturing process.

Now that we understand the objectives, here are the seven steps you need to complete the FMEA process:

1. Document the product or process functions.

2. Determine how the functions could fail (failure modes).

3. Determine how severe the failure consequences (effects) would be.

4. Identify the causes for the failure and their probability of occurrence.

5. List the current methods (controls) of detecting and preventing failures, and the rates of their effectiveness.

6. Assess the risk for each failure.

7. Determine appropriate actions to address the highest-risk failures.

Let me elaborate on these steps. The point of Step 1 is to map out how the product or process is supposed to work, step by step (or function by function).

In Steps 2 and 3, we play devil's advocate and test where the product or process is most vulnerable to failure, how it could fail (e.g., totally, partially, intermittently, and so on), and how severe the failure consequences could be. If a potential failure is deemed trivial (given a 1 rating), it can be discarded from further consideration.

For Step 4, we identify the potential causes for each failure and evaluate the likelihood of occurrence for each cause. Rare failures (1s) need not be considered in the following steps.

Many teams like to evaluate their product or process at this point because the severity and likelihood of the risks have already been analyzed, and those tasks are considered the core of any risk analysis. Other teams save this evaluation for later so that they can proceed to Step 5, the controls phase of the process, where they can give the product or process a detection rating before assessing and prioritizing the risk involved.

In Step 6, we assess the risk for each failure. Finally, and most important, in Step 7, we come up with the appropriate actions needed to minimize or eliminate the potential failures identified earlier. Without this step, of course, the rest isn't worth much.

The FMEA process is obviously a powerful component of the DFSS program, virtually justifying the time, effort, and finances invested in DFSS by itself. Because the entire thrust of DFSS is to design products to achieve a Six Sigma level of quality, it is clearly essential that all serious potential snags are eliminated or contained to allow the product or process to reach that mark. FMEA provides a clear, step-by-step methodology for debugging even very complicated products and processes. And because it is a living document, updated regularly even during production, it documents the lessons learned for all projects that are developed in the future.

To summarize DFSS Phase II, develop concepts: At this stage our task is first to generate many creative solutions to the problem at hand, select the best of the batch, and then do our best to debug it before we proceed. If we do these three tasks well, we'll have a highly innovative, low-risk concept ready to be optimized in Phase III.

One final and very important strategy to keep in mind here: There may be occasions at this stage where the team will go back and use TRIZ to resolve conflicts that are causes of failures. As the team creates "new and improved" concepts, Pugh Concept

Selection Technique will again be utilized to help the team select the most promising concept. FMEA will then be applied to the selected concept. DFSS can be an iterative process, not always just a one-pass exercise.

CHAPTER 6

Optimize the Design

INTRODUCTION TO ROBUST OPTIMIZATION

This is where things get really exciting, because Phase III of DFSS marks a shift from taking in information to making decisions about the information we have and taking action to create something special. Now that we have all our ingredients on the kitchen counter, it's time to start cooking.

In DFSS Phase I, we clearly defined the requirements with target specifications, based on the Voice of the Customer and benchmarking. In other words, we developed consensus on what the new design has to do. Then in Phase II, we selected a concept that has the highest probability of success to meet those requirements.

In Phase III, we are now ready to optimize the design using Robust Design®, a concept as familiar as it is misunderstood. I'll clarify it in this chapter. After Robust Design is completed, Tolerance Design will follow to optimize tolerances at the lowest cost. It is important to note Robust Design is not the same as Tolerance Design. Again, that will be clarified here.

We will conduct Robust Design Optimization by following the famous two-step optimization process created by Dr. Genichi Taguchi:

1. Minimize variability in the product or process (Robust Optimization).

2. Adjust the output to hit the target.

In other words: Let's first optimize the design performance to get the best out of the selected concept, then adjust the output to the target value to confirm if all the requirements are met. The better the concept can perform, the greater our chances to meet all our requirements.

In Step 1, we are trying to kill many birds with just one stone—or many requirements by only doing one thing. How is that possible?

We start the first step of the Robust Design process by identifying the Ideal Function, which will be determined by the basic physics of the system, be it a product or process we're designing. In either case, the design will be evaluated by the basic physics of the system. In the case of evaluating a product or manufacturing process, the ideal function is defined based on an energy transformation from the input to the output. For example, in a car, to go faster the driver presses down the gas pedal and that energy is transformed to increased speed by sending gas through the fuel line to the engine where it's burned and finally to the wheels that turn faster.

Unlike in the design of a product, however, when designing a process, it's not energy that's transformed but information. Take invoicing, for example. The supplier sends the company an invoice and that information starts a chain of events that transforms the information into record keeping and finally a check being sent to the supplier.

In either case, we will first define what the Ideal Function for that particular product or process will look like, then we will seek a design that will minimize the variability of the transformation of energy or information, depending on what we're working on.

We concentrate on the transformation of energy or information because all problems, including defects, failures, and poor reliability, are symptoms of variability in the transformation of energy or information. By optimizing that transformation—taking out virtually all sources of "friction" or noise along the way—we are striving to meet all the requirements at once. We will discuss this in greater detail later in this chapter.

To understand fully Dr. Taguchi's revolutionary approach, let's first review how quality control has traditionally worked. Since virtually the advent of commerce, a "good" or acceptable product or process has been defined simply as one that meets the standards set by the company.

And here's the critical weakness to the old way of thinking: It has always been assumed that ANY product or process that falls ANYWHERE in the acceptable range is equal to any other item that falls within the limits.

You probably can picture the image of the old conveyer belt, where the products roll along the line one by one until they get to the end, where an inspector wearing goggles and a white coat looks at each one and tosses them into either the "acceptable" bin or the "reject" bin. In that factory, there are no other distinctions made among the finished products, just "okay" or "bad."

If you were to ask that old-school inspector what separates the worst "okay" specimen from the best reject—in other words, the ones right near the cut-off line—he'd probably say, "Not much. It's a hair's difference. But you've got to draw the line somewhere." But the inspector treats all acceptable samples the same: He just tosses them in the "okay" bin, and same with the rejects. Even though he knows there are a million shades of gray in the output, he separates them all into black or white.

Now, if you asked a typical consumer of that product if there was any difference between a sample that barely met the standards to make it into the "okay" bin and one that was perfect, she'd say, "Yes, absolutely. You can easily tell the difference between these two."

The difference between the inspector's and the customer's viewpoints can be further clarified with the following analogy: If both people were playing darts, the inspector would only notice if the dart hit the dartboard or not, not caring if it landed near the edge of the board or right on the bull's-eye. But to the customer, there would be a world of difference between the dart that landed on the board's edge, and the one that pierced the bull's-eye. While she certainly wouldn't want any dart not good enough to hit the board, she would still greatly prefer the bull's-eye to the one just an inch inside the board's edge. The point is: With the old way, the manufacturer or service provider made no distinctions among acceptable outputs, but the consumer almost always did, which made the company out of step with the customer's observations and desires.

For example, Figure 6.1 shows the result of 21 field goal trials from 40 yards out by two field goal kickers. Both kickers made all 21, successfully, but which place kicker would you want playing on your team? Easy, isn't it?

This dissonance between these two perspectives demonstrates that the traditional view of quality—"good enough!"—is not good enough in the modern economy. Instead of just barely meeting the lowest possible specifications, we need to hit the

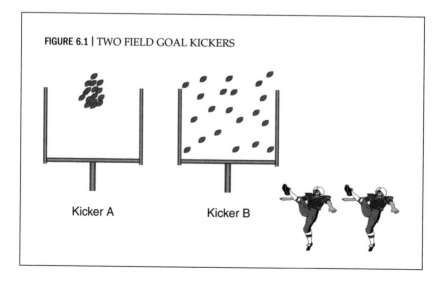

FIGURE 6.1 | TWO FIELD GOAL KICKERS

Kicker A   Kicker B

bull's-eye. The way to do that is to replace the oversimplified over/under bar with a more sophisticated bull's-eye design, where the goal is not merely to make acceptable products, but to reduce the spread of darts around the target.

The same is true on the other side of the mark, too. In the old system, once you meet the specification, that's that. No point going past it. But in DFSS, even if we're already doing a good job on a particular specification, we need to look into whether we can do it better and, if so, what would it cost us? Would improving it pay off?

You might wonder why a company should bother making already good designs into great designs. After all, products don't give out extra credit for exceeding the specifications. Or do they?

DFSS's Robust Design requires you to free your employees—and your imaginations—to achieve the optimum performance by focusing on the energy/information transformation described earlier. This notion of having no ceiling is important not just as a business concept, but psychologically as well. The IRS, of course, tells you how much to pay, and virtually no one ever pays extra. Most taxpayers do their darnedest to pay as little as legally possible. But charities, on the other hand, never tell their donors what to pay—which might explain why Americans are by far the most generous citizens around the world, in terms of charitable giving—dwarfing the percentage of charity funds citizens of other countries commonly give.

The point is simple: Don't give any employee, team, or project an upper limit. Let them optimize and *maximize* the design for robustness. See what's possible, and take advantage of the best performances you can produce! Let the sky be the limit to performance and watch what your people can do! A limitless environment is a very inspiring place to work.

The next big question is this: Once the energy/information transformation is optimized, is the design's performance greater than required? If so, you've got some decisions to make. Let's examine two extreme cases.

When the optimum performance exceeds the requirements then you have plenty of opportunities to reduce real cost. For example, you can use the added value in other ways, by using cheaper materials, increased tolerances, or by speeding up the process. The objective of Robust Design is to improve performance without increasing the cost. Once you can achieve that, you can take advantage of the opportunities that cost reductions can create.

On the flip side, if the optimum performance comes in *below* the requirements, it's time to rethink the concept we selected in Phase II and come up with something better. The problem is that in most corporate cultures it is very difficult to abandon a concept because so many people would have spent so much time and effort on the Project, and would be very reluctant about scrapping it for a new concept.

But this is where leadership comes in. Despite the heartbreak of letting an idea go, if it's not good enough, it's not good enough. So instead of spending good money on a doomed project, fighting the fires later, it's best to cut your losses, reject the concept (salvaging the best ideas, if any), and move on to the next one, instead of locking yourself into a method of production that's never going to give you the results you want. It is extremely important to detect poor designs and reject them at the early stages of development.

Dr. Taguchi has built a model based on this concept that demonstrates the impact that variations from the target have on profits and costs. As the function of the product or process deviates from the target—either above or below it—the quality of the function is compromised. This in turn results in higher losses. The further from the target, the greater the monetary losses will be.

BASELINE PHILOSOPHY: QUALITY LOSS FUNCTION

A tool called the Quality Loss Function (QLF) is very helpful in estimating the overall loss resulting from function deviations from the target. Of course, to make your function more efficient, before you decide to minimize function variation, you need to be sure that the cost to do so is less than the cost would be to maintain the status quo. If you're losing more money from the variations than it would cost to reduce them, you have a very convincing case for taking action. If not, you're better off spending the money elsewhere.

We will refer to the Quality Loss Function in Tolerance Design and decision making in Phase IV. Because Quality Loss Function estimates the cost of functional variations, it is an excellent tool to assist in the decision making that evaluating the cost-performance trade-off requires. We will now show, in detail, how the QLF philosophy can motivate corporations to adopt the culture of Robust Design.

The Quality Loss Function can be put to use for several tasks, including estimating the loss associated with one part of a product or process, the entire item, or even an entire population of products or services if, say, you're looking at something like distribution that affects a wide range of products.

I'll show you how this works mathematically, but don't be discouraged if you're not a math whiz. I'll also show how it works in everyday life, too, which is usually all you'll need to know to do this well.

Let's call the target t. To estimate the loss for a single product or part (or for a service or step, for that matter), we need to determine two things: (1) How far off a product or process is from the target $(y - t)$, and (2) how much that deviation is costing in dollars. We accomplish this by calculating the deviation $(y - t)$, squaring it, and then dividing the dollars lost by that figure. So it looks like this:

$$\frac{D \text{ (Cost of loss in dollars)}}{(y - t)^2} = (k) \text{ Loss coefficient of process}$$

Determining the first sum, the degree of deviation from the norm $(y - t)$ is relatively easy, squaring it presents no problems, but determining the second part of the equation, dollars lost, is much trickier. The reason is, to derive the loss coefficient, we must determine a typical cost of a specific deviation from the target. These two estimates, cost and deviation, will ultimately produce the loss coefficient of the process (k).

Now, here's how it works in everyday life. For an easy example, let's take the old copier paper jam problem. A paper jam is simply a symptom of the variability of energy transformation within the copier. In order for a copy to be unacceptable, the paper displacement rate must not deviate too much, but stay within the realm of $(y - t)$.

When this variability is too great, a copier's performance becomes unacceptable. And when that happens, it will cost the company approximately $300, cost of service and lost productivity for each half day it's out of operation for service.

Now it's time to see how this formula applies to a small number of products (or processes) with various deviations from the target. Those outputs that hit the target will cost the company no losses (apart from the original production costs), while those that lie further and further from the target cost the company more and more money.

One simple way to estimate the average loss per product is to total the individual offset deviations, square the sum, then divide by the number of products, and finally multiply the resulting figure by the loss coefficient (k).

When you compare the average loss of the function to one with a "tighter" deviation, you will quickly see that the average loss of the second group would be much less. And that's the idea.

Having covered how to calculate deviation, loss, average loss, and the loss coefficient, now we need to ask the fundamental question: What creates the variation in our products and processes in the first place? Solve that puzzle, and we can adjust that variation as we see fit.

NOISE FACTORS

The bugaboos that create the wiggles in the products and processes we create can be separated into the following general categories:

- Manufacturing variation, material variation, assembly variation

- Environmental influences (not ecological, but atmospheric)

- Customer causes

- Deterioration, aging, and wear

- Neighboring subsystems

This list will become especially important to us when we embark upon the Parameter Design for Robust Optimization, whose stated purpose is to minimize the system's sensitivity to these sources of variation. From here on, we will lump ALL these sources and their categories under the all-encompassing title of noise, meaning not just unwanted sound, but anything that prevents the product or process from functioning as a smooth, seamless entity. Think of it as the friction that gets in the way of perfect performance.

When DFSS teams confront a function beset with excessive variation caused by noises, the worst possible response is to ignore the problem and hope no one notices—the slip-it-under-the-rug response. Needless to say, this never solves the problem, but it is a surprisingly common response.

As you might expect, more proactive teams usually respond by either attacking the sources of the noise, trying to buffer them, or compensating for the noise by other means. All these approaches can work to a degree, depending on the exact situation, but they will almost always add to the cost of the product or process.

Traditionally, companies have created new products and processes by the simple formula design-build-test, or, essentially, trial and error. This has its appeal, of course, but is ultimately time-consuming, inefficient, and unimaginative. It's physically rigorous, but intellectually lazy.

PARAMETER DESIGN

Robust Design takes a different approach. Instead of the solutions above, which all kick in AFTER the noise is discovered, Parameter Design works to eliminate the effect of noise BEFORE it occurs, by making the function immune to the sources of variation. It's the difference between prevention and cure—one of the biggest themes of DFSS. (Parameter Design is another name for Robust Design, a design parameter optimization for robustness.)

We accomplish this by identifying design factors we can control, and exploit those factors to minimize or eliminate the negative effects of any possible deviations—sort of like finding a natural predator for a species that's harming crops and people. Instead of battling the species directly with pesticides and the like, it's more efficient to find another agent to do it for you naturally.

The first step to doing this is to discard the familiar approach to quality control, which really is a focus on failure, in favor of a new approach that focuses on SUCCESS.

Instead of coming up with the countless ways a system might go wrong, analyzing those failures, and applying a countermeasure for each potential failure, we will focus on the much smaller number of ways we can make things go right! It's much faster to think that way, and much more rewarding, too. Think of the world of scientists versus engineers. It is the goal of scientists to understand the entire world, even the universe, inside and out. A noble goal, surely, but not a very efficient one. It is the engineer's goal, however, simply to understand what he needs to understand to make the product or process he's working on

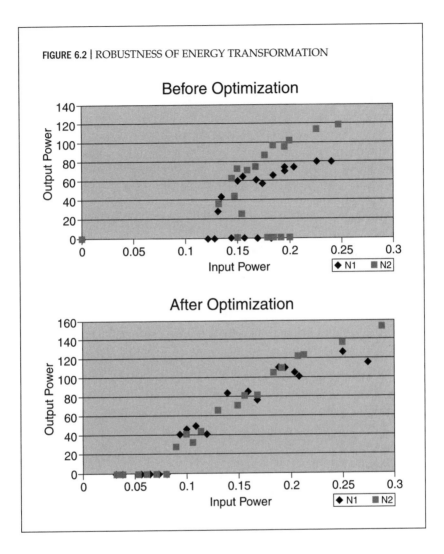

FIGURE 6.2 | ROBUSTNESS OF ENERGY TRANSFORMATION

work well. In this comparison, *we need to think like engineers, looking for solutions, not like pure scientists, looking for explanations for every potential problem.*

The usual quality control systems try to determine the symptoms of poor quality, track the rate of failure in the product or process, then attempt to find out what's wrong and how to fix it. It's a backwards process, where you begin with failure and trace it back to how it occurred.

In Parameter Design, we take a different tack—one that may seem a little foreign at first, but is ultimately much more rewarding and effective. As I've already explained, every product or process ultimately boils down to a system where energy is transferred from one thing to another to create that product or process. It's how electricity becomes a cool breeze pumping out of your air conditioner. (In the case of software or business processes, as I mentioned earlier, a system transforms information, not energy, and exactly the same optimization can be applied.)

In the Parameter Design approach, instead of analyzing failure modes of an AC unit, we measure and optimize the variability and efficiency of the energy transformation from the socket to the cool air pumping out of the unit. In other words, we optimize the quality of energy transformation, as illustrated in Figure 6.2.

This forces us to clearly define each intended function so we can reduce its variability and maximize its efficiency. In fact, that's another core issue of Parameter Design: shifting from focusing on what's wrong and how to fix it, to focusing on what's right and how to maximize it. Mere debugging and bandaging are not always the most effective ways.

To gain a deeper understanding of the distinctions between the old and new ways of thinking on this point, it might be helpful to walk through an example. Let's look at the transfer case of a brand new four-wheel-drive truck. Now, as you probably know, the basic function of this system is as follows: The fuel system sends fuel to the engine, which turns it into active energy and sends it on to the transmission, which sends it on to the transfer case, whose job is to take that energy and distribute it to the front and rear axles for maximum traction and power. The transfer case, therefore, acts as the clearinghouse, or distribution center, for the car's energy.

Even with new transfer cases, common problems include: audible noise, excessive vibration, excessive heat generation, poor driving feel, premature failure or breakdown, and poor reliability. When engineers see any of these conditions, they traditionally have jumped right in to modify the transfer case's design to minimize the particular problem. The catch is, however, that oftentimes "fixing" one of these problems only makes another one worse. For example, we could reduce audible noise, only to find a dangerous increase in friction-generated heat.

It's like squeezing one end of a balloon only to see the other end expand, or quitting smoking only to see your weight increase. Using this approach, instead of eradicating the problem, we've only shifted the symptom of variability from one area to another—and spent a lot of time, energy, and money in the process.

With Parameter Design, however, instead of trying to debug the transfer case bug by bug, which often results in us chasing our tail, we focus on reducing the variability of energy transformation then maximizing the energy that goes through the transfer case cleanly. In other words, we shift our focus from defense to offense.

The theory goes like this: If we could create a perfect transfer case with zero energy loss, there would be no "wasted" energy necessary to create audible noise, heat, vibration, and so on. Sounds good, of course, but obviously building the perfect transfer case is still a pipe dream. But the thinking behind the perfect transfer case, however, can help us build a better one. Wouldn't it be better to try to achieve the perfect energy-efficient transfer case, than to try to achieve perfection through endless debugging, putting out fire after fire in the hopes of eliminating fires forever? As Ben Franklin said, "An ounce of prevention is worth a pound of cure." We try to build that prevention into the design. It's estimated that in a typical U.S. company, engineers spend 80 percent of their time putting out fires, not preventing them. Smart companies reverse this ratio.

Usually, the single biggest source of function variation stems from how the customer uses the product or process. (Recall noise factors.) The reason is simple: Labs are sterile places where sensible scientists test the product or process under reasonable conditions, but customers can use these products in a thousand different ways and environments, adding countless variables, including aging and wear. Virtually no one can anticipate the many ways customers might be tempted to use the product or process. This is how we get warning labels on lawn mowers advising consumers not to use them on hedges.

But that's the real world. We cannot prevent customers from using their four-wheel-drive cars in just about any manner they wish. So, how do we solve this problem?

Let's take a simple pair of scissors as an example. When designed well, as almost all of them are, they can cut regular paper and basic cloth well enough. But what can you do about customers who buy them to use on materials for which they were never intended, such as leather or plastic?

Most companies would do one of two things. Either they include stern warnings in the owner's manual and on the product itself that the scissors are not intended for use on leather or plastic, and that using them on those materials will render the warranty null and void. Or, companies can give up trying to educate the customers, assume the worst, and bolster the design of the scissors so they actually can cut leather and plastic.

The problem with the first approach is that such warnings only go so far; your company might still be found liable in court. And, in any case, even intelligent customers might be turned off by a pair of scissors that cannot cut through leather and plastic, even if they never intend to use theirs in that way. The problem with the second approach—making the scissors all but bulletproof—is that for the vast majority of customers, the extra materials and joint-strengthening are overkill, and will raise the price of the product even for people who will never need such additional force.

With Parameter Design, however, you don't need to resort to either unsatisfactory solution, because the method helps you create "perfect scissors" that require virtually no effort to cut almost any material. Instead of simply bolstering the device, Parameter Design streamlines the product to avoid the problems that arise when it's being used on tough materials—much the way offices solved their "paper problem" not by merely building more and bigger file cabinets, but by converting their information to microfilm, microfiche, and, finally, computer disks.

Making the scissors more efficient reduces the odds of damage and deterioration, and, therefore effectively makes the scissors immune to the extremes of customer use variation—without burdening the product with undue costs.

The same concept of Parameter Design for Robust Optimization can be applied to the design of a business transactional process. Let's take efficiency of hospital service, for example. Even for a case like this, we can look at the system as an energy transformation.

Each patient visiting an ER represents the input to the system. Every one of them has a different level of demands. One may require a simple diagnosis and a prescription, another patient may require immediate surgery. The total time spent by a patient in the hospital represents the output. Therefore, we can define the Ideal Function as the ideal relationship between the input demanded and the actual output. Then we want to optimize the system for robustness. We want the relationship between the input and output to have the least variability at the highest efficiency.

In other words, we want the design to address the number of beds, number of nurse staff, number of health unit coordination on staff, number of doctors on staff, pharmacy hours of in-house coverage, ER coordinator, dedicated X-ray services, private triage space, etc. And we want the design to be the most robust against noise factors such as: total number of patients visited, time of patient visit, equipment down time, lab delay, private MD delay, absenteeism, etc.

In essence, we want the relationship between the inputs (the demands of each patient) and the outputs (the time spent on each patient) to have the smallest variability with the highest efficiency.

Next, we formulate an experiment with this objective in mind, which can be executed by computer simulation instead of more expensive, real life models.

The eight key steps of Parameter Design are:

1. Define the scope. Define which system/subsystem you are optimizing.

2. Define the Ideal Function.

3. Develop the strategy for how you are going to induce the effect of noises.

4. Determine design parameters and their alternative levels.

5. Conduct the test/simulation to obtain data.

6. Analyze the data using the signal-to-noise ratio, a metric for robustness.

7. Predict the performance of optimum design.

8. Conduct a confirmation trial using the optimum design.

In summary, in Phase III DFSS, teams will learn how to apply the principles of Dr. Taguchi's Parameter Design to optimize the performance of a given system in a far more elegant fashion than just debugging or bolstering it would ever accomplish.

TOLERANCE DESIGN

In Parameter Design, we optimize the design for robustness by selecting design parameter values, which means defining the materials, configurations, and dimensions needed for the design. For a transfer case in a four-wheel-drive truck, for example, we will define the type of gears needed, the gear material, the gear heat treatment method, the shaft diameter, and so on. For a hospital, we would define the number of beds, pharmacy hours, etc. So you can see that, in Parameter Design, we define the nominal values that will determine the design.

The next step is Tolerance Design, in which we'll optimize our tolerances for maximum effect—which does NOT necessarily mean making them all as tight as they can be. What it DOES mean is making them tight where they need to be tight, and allowing looser ones where we can afford to have looser ones, thus maximizing the quality, efficiency, and thrift of our design.

For Tolerance Design optimization, we will use the Taguchi Quality Loss Function (QLF) to help us evaluate the effectiveness of changing dimensional or material tolerances. This allows us to see if our results are better or worse as we tweak a particular element up or down.

Let's start with Tolerance Design optimization. Tolerancing is a generic label often applied to any method of setting tolerances, be they tolerances for dimensions, materials, or time, in the case of a process.

Tolerance Design means something more specific: a logical approach to establishing the appropriate tolerances based on their overall effect on system function (sensitivity) and what it costs to control. As mentioned above, the key model employed in Tolerance Design is Taguchi's Quality Loss Function, or QLF. To say it another way, Tolerance Design describes a specific approach to improve tolerances by tightening up the most critical tolerances (not ALL of them, in other words) at the lowest possible cost through the QLF.

This requires us first to determine which tolerances have the greatest impact on the system variability, which we accomplish by designing experiments using orthogonal arrays. This experiment is done by computer simulation (occasionally by a hardware). This will allow us to prioritize our tolerances—to decide which changes reap the greatest rewards—and thereby help us make wise decisions about the status of our various options, letting us know which ones we should tighten, loosen, or leave alone.

Think of it as a baseball team's batting order, and you're the manager. Your job is to maximize run production, and you do it by trying different players in different spots in the lineup. The key is isolating who helps and who doesn't. Substituting various players in the lineup and changing the order will give you the results you need to determine who works best and where.

This brings us to the six DFSS Tolerance Design steps:

1. Determine the Quality Loss Function (QLF).

2. Design and run (or simulate) the experiment to determine the percent contribution of each tolerance.

3. Determine tolerance upgrading action plan and estimate its cost for each of the high contributors.

4. Determine tolerance degrading action plan for the no/low-contributing tolerances and estimate its cost reduction.

5. Finalize your tolerance upgrading and degrading action plan based on the percentage of contribution, quality loss, and the cost.

6. Confirm the effectiveness of your plan.

The DFSS approach to Tolerance Design will help teams meet one of the primary objectives of the program, namely developing a product or process with Six Sigma quality while keeping costs to a minimum. The steps above are intended to help you and your team work through the process of establishing optimal tolerances for optimal effect.

The goal is not simply to tighten every standard, but to make more sophisticated decisions about tolerances. To clarify what we mean by this, let's consider a sports analogy.

Billy Martin was a good baseball player and a great manager. He had his own off-field problems, but as a field general, he had no equal. One of the reasons he was so good was because he was smart enough first to see what kind of team he had, THEN to find a way to win with them, playing to their strengths and covering their weaknesses—unlike most coaches, who have only one approach that sometimes doesn't mesh with their players.

In the 1970s, when he was managing the Detroit Tigers, a big slow team, he emphasized power—extra base hits and home runs. When he coached the Oakland A's a decade later, however, he realized that team could never match Detroit's home run power, but they were fast, so he switched his emphasis from big hits to base stealing, bunting, and hitting singles. In both places, he won division crowns, but with very different teams.

It's the same with DFSS Tolerance Design. We don't impose upon the product or process what we think should happen. We look at what we have, surmise what improvements will get the best results, and test our theories. In Detroit, Martin didn't bother trying to make his team faster and steal more bases because it wouldn't have worked. He made them focus on hitting even more home runs, and they did. In Oakland, he didn't make them lift weights and try to hit more homers, because they didn't have that ability. He made them get leaner and meaner and faster, and steal even more bases. And that's why it worked: he played to his teams' strengths.

You don't want to spend any money to upgrade low-contributing tolerances. You want to reduce cost by taking advantage of these tolerances. For a high-contributing tolerance, you don't want to upgrade it if it is too expensive. If the price is right, you will upgrade those high contributors. Tolerance Design is all about balancing COST against PERFORMANCE and QUALITY.

CONCEPTUAL DESIGN, PARAMETER DESIGN, THEN TOLERANCE DESIGN

In DFSS, it is extremely important to follow the steps as shown in Figure 6.3.

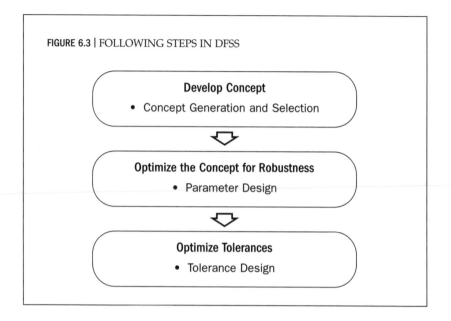

FIGURE 6.3 | FOLLOWING STEPS IN DFSS

Develop Concept
- Concept Generation and Selection

Optimize the Concept for Robustness
- Parameter Design

Optimize Tolerances
- Tolerance Design

One common problem is that people skip Parameter Design and conduct Tolerance Design. You should be aware of the opportunities you are missing if you skip Parameter Design.

By skipping Parameter Design:

- You are missing great opportunities for cost reduction. You are getting the best the concept can perform by optimizing for robustness. If the best is far better than requirements, there are plenty of opportunities to reduce cost.

- You are missing the opportunity to find a bad concept, so that you reject the bad concept at the early stage of product/process development. If the best concept you can do is not good enough, you have to change the concept.

The result of Tolerance Design on designs that have not been optimized is far different from the result of Tolerance Design after robust optimization has taken place. In other words, you end up with tightening tolerances, which would have been unnecessary if the design was optimized for robustness in the first place. Think of all fire-fighting activities your company is doing today. If the design was optimized, you would have fewer problems and the problems would be different. Hence, solutions are different.

CHAPTER 7

Verify
the Design

In Phase I, we defined our opportunities for improvements, captured the Voice of the Customer with imaginative understanding of the customer's needs, and came up with a rough plan for success. In Phase II, we considered several design concepts and settled on the most appealing one. In Phase III, we optimized our design performance through Robust Design®, namely Parameter Design and Tolerance Design. Now in Phase IV, we will verify that design by confirming that it's working as we had hoped.

In Phase IV, we will verify the design, validate our process, establish process controls, complete a formal cost-benefit analysis and "capture" the lessons learned. Needless to say, Phase IV is a busy one. It is also one of the most rewarding, as we get to see the puzzle take shape, and begin to reap the fruits of our efforts.

After we do our work, we need to verify our design by testing it. There are several good reasons to do this:

- Some verifications are required by law, for consumer protection, environmental protections, and other legal concerns. There's no point in questioning these requirements—we might as well curse the darkness—but it is possible to question any specifications we may have that exceed legal requirements.

147

- Verifications can be helpful if we're not completely sure if our designs will meet our required specifications. The contrapositive proves the need for this: if we knew for sure our design would meet all our specifications, we wouldn't need to keep testing it.

- Verifications also can be helpful if it turns out that our preliminary tests don't have much correlation with real world applications of the product or process. This will help us shift from a focus on testing to a focus on verification—not the same thing. When testing, of course, we're not sure what to expect, and that's why we test. But when we're verifying the results, we're simply confirming that our expectations are being met. We must verify that there are no serious, unexpected side effects.

A few rules of thumb apply here. One of the pillars of DFSS, and one of the things that distinguishes DFSS from other quality initiatives, is our emphasis on baking quality into the design, not trying to squeeze it back into the mix after it comes out of the oven through trial-and-error methods. This saves time and money, and makes for a more "solid," built-in quality than other systems can offer. As we all know, but don't always practice, quality cannot be tested in, it must be built in.

This leads to a central thesis of DFSS, a central rule of thumb, namely that both product and process designs must be completed prior to verification. Verification is all too often used as just another step in the design process rather than VERIFICATION of completed product and process designs. The process of managing by the calendar rather than excellence of execution of the DFSS process is the central cause of expensive, inefficient, ineffective, and time-consuming fire fighting and delayed launches of less-than-world-class products and services.

We will verify functional performances and do our best to make our tests representative of the real world situations our products and processes will face. Finally, we will strive to bolster engineering confidence in our plans, products, and processes to ensure shortfalls in quality do not reach our customers.

To accomplish this vital list of goals, we'll need to address several general issues surrounding the verification process, such as:

- How close were the prototypes to the real thing?

- How did we determine the functional requirements?

- How accurately was the application environment defined?

- How was the predicted useful life of the product or process determined?

As you might imagine, each time we move on to the next phase, our work in the previous phase(s) becomes more important. By the fourth and final phase, we have to rely on the quality of our work in three previous phases. Everything we've surveyed and analyzed and decided before—including the corporate objectives, customer desires and uses, competitive trends, and government regulations—will shape our final outcome in Phase IV. Phase IV is the stage to test the design to verify it is meeting all requirements, instead of the typical test-to-find-problems approach.

As we've said throughout this book, the DFSS difference is that we do not merely "tack on" as much quality as we can afford after creating the product or process, we design it into the commodity from the start, and build the rest around it. But this is not easy. We use DFSS-QFD to help us understand the requirements we decide are essential, then we use those requirements to verify that what we've made satisfies our original intent.

In Phase IV, we use many of the outcomes from the previous phases and tasks. In addition to checking to be sure we've satisfied the DFSS-QFD requirements, we also check to be sure that the high-priority failure modes and causes identified in the DFSS-FMEA process have been resolved, too. And finally, we "capture" our results in a report so supervisors can check our work and sign off on it.

THE THREE STEPS TO VERIFYING THE DESIGN

The three steps in the verification of DFSS Projects are:

1. Verify the capability of the manufacturing process.

2. Conduct the prototype build-test-fix cycle.

3. Conduct a pilot production run.

The first step, verifying the capability of manufacturing processes, entails establishing and confirming the capability of personnel, training processes, manufacturing processes and controls, equipment, gauges, measurement systems, and calibration procedures to deliver flawless products at the lowest possible cost.

This is primarily the work of manufacturing professionals supported by engineering professionals. While the methodologies are well known within manufacturing environments, DFSS places significantly tougher demands on the quality with which this work needs to be executed. Traditional standards of excellence are no longer adequate to deliver Six Sigma quality. The details are an integral part of DFSS.

The second step, conducting the prototype build-test-fix cycle, is a central activity that brings engineering, manufacturing, and service personnel together with customers to verify delivery of superior quality and lower cost products and services that delight customers more than competitive offerings.

There are many ways to verify our work, of course, but one of the most innovative is called *Test to Bogey*. In this approach, you determine a minimum acceptance point for the function's performance and establish a useful-life bogey (usually measured in time or cycles), then set up a test and run it. If enough prototypes succeed, you can proclaim the design a success.

To Test to Bogey effectively, you need to determine how many prototypes need to be tested to make it a fair test. This requires balancing the need for a good sample size with the extra time and money it costs to increase the pool of prototypes. In the rare case that all the prototypes pass the test, you need to determine if they have been overdesigned— that is, made better than they have to be. If you're trying to build the ultimate SUV, for example, a tank will more than exceed the four-wheel-drive requirements, but probably represents overkill—and excess cost.

When that happens, it can be helpful to explore the situation more fully via a new tool, *Test to Failure.* In this system, you test all prototypes until they ALL FAIL, which is how you separate the men from the boys. In much the way demanding coaches and teachers do, if you give your prototypes a very tough test, you can spread them out along the spectrum. Then you can study which ones perform the best and why.

Like Goldilocks, you may find a third version is juuuuust right. The weakness of Test to Bogey is that it measures only stamina. Test to Failure measures only performance. But a third approach, called *Functional Degradation Testing (FDT),* measures the performance AND stamina—which is what customers measure, too. This entails charting the product's or process's erosion over a set period of time. The advantages are several: FDT does not require as large a sample size as the first two, yet still provides much more information about the design than either Test to Bogey or Test to Failure.

Of course, FDT also presents several challenges, too, including determining what performance levels would satisfy customers over the useful life of the product or process. (Keeping in mind that most customers will accept a decline in performance of most products and processes over time, including cars and electronics, for example.) Another challenge is measuring the performance without affecting the future measures—in other words, how do you test a car thoroughly without taking away some of its longevity?

In short, the three steps of FDT looks like this:

1. Determine the length of a useful product or process life.

2. Establish an acceptable performance level over the course of that life.

3. Evaluate the prototype product's/process's function over time.

This is how this system combines the best of both the Test to Bogey and the Test to Failure. Instead of just measuring one axis or the other, FDT measures both, giving more sophisticated and accurate readings.

FDT is not fooled by fast starters. It is impressed only by those products and processes that hold up well over time. In other words, products and processes that maintain strong performances for long periods—and that's how you test for robustness!

On the other hand, a form of FDT can be done with the robustness metric of Robust Design. This can be applied when a current or existing design with known performance is available. Here, instead of optimizing a design, we will only assess the robustness of the new design against the known design. For example, a current transfer case design and the new design will be assessed for robustness of their energy transformation. We will expose both the new and known design to the same effectively chosen noise conditions. If the measured robustness of the new design is twice as good as the known design, we will conclude the failure rate would be half or better.

Of course, all three of these tests—Test to Bogey, Test to Failure, and Functional Degradation Testing—test DESIGN. While DFSS is naturally concerned with testing design, we must also test for the manufacturing or service PROCESS. After all, if we cannot produce the design we just finished testing at the specified volume, quality, and cost levels, it's just a fancy prototype we can show off but never sell. This test turns dreams into reality. This leads to the third step of verification.

The third verification step is to conduct a pilot production run to verify the capability of manufacturing and assembly processes to deliver design intent with high quality at the lowest possible costs.

The pilot production run is a test to prove that the products we make from the production tools and processes meet the requirements established earlier. After we validate the process, we are ready to "lock it down" by instituting controls to ensure that the process we've tested can continue to produce consistently good products. This marks a fundamental shift in our thinking, from simply focusing on defining the product characteristics to identifying the precise process conditions that create consistently good products. This also tells us what process variables we'll need to control to ensure we can continue to produce great products and processes.

To review with an example: If we are building a car, we will build several prototypes for testing. First, in Test to Bogey, we will see how they perform during one month of hard driving, and examine the ones that met our standards and those that did not. Then we will Test to Failure to see how long they can maintain our standards—this time examining those that lasted a long time and those that quickly fell below standards. Finally, we will subject the prototypes to Functional Degradation Testing to see which prototypes have the best combination of stamina and quality, and why. When we finish with that, we will undertake a pilot production run, to make sure we can manufacture what are sometimes called production prototypes on a grand scale, mimicking the manufacturing process again and again. For example, what conditions make for the best paint jobs, and how can we duplicate the humidity and temperature levels to guarantee success every time?

PROCESS CONTROL

This brings us to *Process Control,* one of the last stages of our work on DFSS. This is a system of actions designed to maintain our process performance at a level that satisfies customers' needs and also drives the ongoing improvement. This is where we secure all the gains we've made in the four phases of DFSS to ensure that we remember them and can duplicate them.

To "freeze" our progress and allow others to build on it, we must first standardize the tasks we performed to create our success in the first place. (These standardizations need not require perfection, of course, but should be sufficiently uniform that we can establish an accurate baseline with them, as can future generations.) Then we must document the new procedures and instructions so that even those who were not part of the original discussions can perform them well by themselves—making it a sort of company-specific DFSS training manual.

Then the *Process Control plan* will identify key measurements, so others can check their work along the way like a recipe, plus adjustments needed and tasks that require special controls. As the project matures, these special controls should be replaced by either designing them out of the process, error-proofing them, or replacing them with visual controls.

The final step entails determining what to do if a control fails when used later—or if anything else in the plan fails to work as it previously did. This additional information will be stored in the Response plan, which we will discuss later.

Now, more specifically, there are some things to consider when standardizing the process. One of the first questions almost every team will ask in Phase IV is how specific must their standardizations be. You don't want to be so vague that a colleague reading your work can't understand what to do next, but you also don't want to be so specific that it takes forever to read your instructions.

You might consider this our own customized constitution. Our forefathers did incredibly heroic and noble work to earn our freedom, but unless they recorded their new system in writing, we would never be able to follow it for future generations. In order to maintain our gains, they had to create a system that could duplicate their ideas of freedom and justice.

For them it was the Constitution. In DFSS it is a Process Control plan. We need a Process Control plan because without a formal control mechanism, our purified processes would degrade or drift away in the wrong direction. Only by establishing a formal, measurable control process can we sustain our improvements, and even enhance them over time. If our forefathers didn't write down the formula for freedom, if the inventors of baseball didn't establish the magical rules, and if Einstein never recorded his theories in words and numbers, we would never be able to draw on their great work.

On an everyday level, you can think of it as a recipe. Instead of letting others try to duplicate your great dish using their instincts and savvy, you want to write it down so the meal doesn't die with you. And you need to do it well enough that someone who has never met you can duplicate the dish to perfection.

Exactly how detailed your directions need to be depends on several factors:

- How much risk is involved if the reader does the wrong thing?

- What is the target audience's need for details, and its tolerance of ambiguity?

- How much of an impact will additional factors like job turnover have on the project in the future? The greater the turnover, the less you can take for granted in writing the Process Control plan.

Think of it in terms of directions to a destination. Your visitor doesn't need or want a detailed account of every square foot of road, but he does need to know the crucial signs and instructions that will lead him to your home. You need to determine the vital "cross roads," and the telltale "signs" that will most effectively guide others to the destination. And that's a skill, as much as an art.

Now, let's get the rubber to the road. When it's time to put all this into motion, here's an important point to remember: when standardizing a production or service process, it is vital that those who will be doing the jobs lead the way. This gives them ownership of the process—as opposed to having it forced upon them, with inevitably negative results—and it also greatly increases the accuracy and usability of the Process Control plan. The reason is simple: The people who do the work the most are the people who know it the best. If you forget that, you'll fall into the trap of top-down management, where the people making the most detailed decisions have the least firsthand expertise making those decisions. And last, if there is turnover in the position and the workers who wrote the instructions are no longer the people doing the work they wrote about, the new employees will recognize immediately that the author of the instructions had done their job. Credibility will be instantaneous.

When the team members are ready to commit the job task to a permanent form of recording, they should feel free to consider several options for communicating their message. These can include the old standby, written text, or a graphic approach using depictions—drawings or actual photos—especially if the task is highly technical and detailed, such as machine work. They might also elect to communicate the job standards through a three-dimensional model, videotaped instructions, or a computer-based program. The point is that they should take the time to consider all the possibilities, and pick the one they think best suits the task in question.

Like everything else we do in DFSS, they should also keep the customer in mind at all times—in this case, the internal customer who will be receiving the information they present. They should test out early editions of their work on the very people who will be absorbing it later on to see what hits the mark and what is confusing.

GETTING DOWN TO BUSINESS

When the team sits down to sort out its message, it forces the members to think more thoroughly on the process itself. This is one of the hidden benefits of writing and other forms of communication. As they say, you don't know what you're trying to say until after you've already said it. Luckily, in writing, filmmaking, and so on, you can return to it, revise it, and say it better before the audience sees it. The process itself requires clearer thinking than just doing the job, so it helps us understand the thing we're talking about that much better.

For example, in this case, sitting down to produce our procedures manual will force us to consider what should be controlled, and by whom. The team's first thoughts on this topic will likely center around *inputs*—the materials, resources, and data required to deliver the output successfully. And one of the team's first concerns about inputs will probably be the quality of the inputs to the process. Over time, however, a good DFSS goal is to ensure that the providers of these inputs do such a consistently good job that it is no longer necessary for the recipient to inspect them before putting them to use. Inputs should be controlled at the source, not at the point of input. This saves time and money while improving quality, thereby representing a classic DFSS approach to quality control.

After inputs comes the *process*, where, obviously enough, the focus of the Process Control rightly belongs. There is no shortage of items that CAN be controlled at this level, so the challenge is deciding which tasks are worthy of special controls and which ones don't need extra attention. This is essentially a triage process, where we COULD fiddle with every item, but should wisely decide which ones need our attention, and which ones are "goners," that is, in this case, those that don't require intensive DFSS treatment.

The best way to sort these out, fortunately, is a process with which you're already quite familiar: Parameter Design, in which we design experiments to test each task and use the test results to separate them into different categories. This will help us understand more clearly the limits of each task, and define them to the point where we can clearly document each input's influence on the output, and therefore know where we can allow variations and how much. This is equivalent to understanding a recipe so well you know what ingredients and tasks you can substitute for or adjust, and which ones are inflexible. (Parameters that do not substantially affect the final product but are necessary for safety or regulatory reasons should also be subjected to special controls.)

Next comes the *output* itself, which is, as you would guess, the tangible product or service we provide our customers—internal or external. It may surprise you to learn that these outputs are NOT the focus of any particular controls in the DFSS system. This is another core philosophy of DFSS: If we take care of our work upstream, we don't have to worry too much about what flows out of the river into the sea. But they can help us think about what process parameters further upstream merit special controls.

Generally speaking, an effective approach to Process Control is to start with the end in mind—that is, the final product or process parameters, derived from the customer's needs and expectations—and work BACKWARDS to institute the necessary process variables to create that outcome. To do this, a tool called the *Statistical Process Control* (SPC) can be very helpful. The SPC observes patterns in the output variations, and connects those patterns with changes in the process conditions, which allows us to determine which process variables influence the output and how, and which ones don't, which in turn tells us which factors are candidates for special controls and which are not.

Again, back to the recipe. If we experiment with it enough times, we'll discover which ingredients—and how much of each—influence the taste and texture of the final product and which ones don't. And this allows us to streamline the recipe because we know which elements are vital to a good outcome and which are not.

Too often, SPC is viewed merely as a charting exercise, only useful to determine if the process is operating as intended. But this sells the entire SPC concept short. The purpose of the charts it creates is to help us understand the sources of the outcome variation, so that their sources can be managed. While SPC can be used to identify special causes of variation, and thereby prompt action—like setting up a quarantine of all affected units, or the elimination of a certain input—its biggest value is derived from the data patterns it reveals, which you can then connect to the various process conditions. SPC is a highly effective means to gauge which variations affect the process and which don't.

The ultimate goal is to eliminate as many of the special controls as possible by making the product or process error-proof, redesigning it, or instituting visual controls that all but do the job for us.

Error-proofing is one of the most effective ways to eliminate these special controls, and it's a one-time-only cost. Special controls, on the other hand, generally take more time and cost more money for the entire life of the production run—a sort of tax you have to pay every day the product or process is up and going. Each time you find a way to eliminate one of those special controls, therefore, you pay for the removal once, but the move pays dividends every day thereafter. It's the difference between paying cash for a car and financing one. The one-time hit may be costly, but after that, you're saving money.

Everyday consumer products have lots of error-proofing designs in them, and are easy to understand. The manufacturer's first challenge is to eliminate the possibility of the customer operating the product or process incorrectly, even dangerously. This is what gives us safety guards on circular saws, cars that won't start unless they're in park, and three-pronged electrical plugs. The trick is to apply these generic concepts of error-proofing to YOUR products and processes. The second step is automating all or part of high-risk processes, in the hopes of reducing the impact human error can have.

Third, look to facilitate correct operation of your products and processes. You can accomplish this softer form of error-proofing (really, error-minimizing) by making each task simpler and more natural to perform. Take self-serve gas stations, an idea that seemed impossibly dangerous and ill-advised three decades ago. It has since been made virtually error-proof. How'd they do it? Clear, simple instructions on the pump. A "safety" handle that shuts itself off when the tank is full. And, if you're silly enough to drive off with the nozzle still in your tank, the hose releases and the flow of gas is shut off to that hose automatically.

Almost any process can be made safer through color-coding and visual controls. Why do you suppose go is always green, stop is red, and every traffic sign has its own unique shape and color? These measures let you know immediately if you're looking at a construction situation or a yield, without even having to read the sign. You usually can tell what kind of sign it is even when viewed from behind, based on its shape alone.

Finally, you also can reduce errors by distinguishing all aspects of the product or process so they can only be used for one thing, the one you intend. That's why plugs are made with one wider prong and one narrower one, so they can only go in certain sockets, thus ensuring electrical safety.

Once you have an effective process control system in place, you can easily determine when one aspect of it gets out of line.

If you have clearly defined tracks, you know when the train is off line and you can figure out exactly where it got off the straight and narrow. Thus, with a good process control system, you've got a built-in system for identifying and correcting any unexpected problems that arise.

If your company is still stuck in the "monitoring output" stage where the guy in the white coat at the end of the conveyer belt looks at the product and then tosses it in the okay or not-okay bin, then it will be more difficult to establish a more effective, more sophisticated approach as we've outlined here. First you must quarantine all suspect products or processes to examine them to determine what went wrong. This is not as easy as it sounds because there could be countless sources of flaws to investigate—as many potential spawning grounds as there are mistakes to examine.

As we prepare to close out the fourth and final phase of DFSS, it's time to recalculate the cost benefit of the project—a sort of midterm grade on our work. (The final cost-benefit analysis cannot be completed until the product retires, because even though we should have solid cost data, some of the data on benefits will be based on projections we can't verify until the product life runs its course.)

Fortunately, we do have the first-pass benefit numbers we calculated in Phase I of the process. These figures can be used as a baseline to compare our latest cost-benefit numbers. By comparing the actual time, costs, and quality returns to those figures in the baseline, we will be able to get a more thorough and accurate estimate of the benefits we can expect to reap from the DFSS methodology. At this juncture we can also make fair estimates of volume projections, long-term manufacturing cost reductions, and service and support costs.

The final task of the DFSS program is to capture the lessons learned, because if we don't, all the wisdom gained will be lost to the next team and the next Project it pursues. While it might be easier to move on without this step—it almost seems like an afterthought—its tremendous value will be as obvious as that of the Rosetta Stone to future DFSS team members.

To break it down, we need to capture the lessons learned with each tool and method applied, and with each function and discipline. Do this well, and this information will provide the feed-forward control system for future Projects, and, not least, will allow all these "secrets" to be owned by the Champion, thus assuring that it will not be pushed aside in favor of a new fad that will inevitably come down the pike.

THE REST OF THE STORY

DFSS Projects often focus on a portion of a product and service offering. A Project may involve the redesign of a troublesome portion of a product or service or a critical element of a new product introduction or new service introduction. In these cases, the efforts of a Project team must be coordinated with the larger program activities.

The verification phase of new product or service introductions continues through launch and ramp-up, and tracking and improving performance under actual customer usage conditions in the field. These activities are managed and carried out by launch teams with support from the DFSS Project teams as needed. Intense participation of the DFSS teams usually ends with the prototype build-test–fix cycle and a hand-off to the downstream process owners.

Corporations that have been engaged in DFSS for some period of time such as GE have gone further to rebuild their new product and process introduction processes on the solid foundation of Design for Six Sigma. Recall the quotes from GE's 1998 annual report:

Every new GE product and service in the future will be DFSS—Designed for Six Sigma. These new offerings will truly take us to a new definition of "World Class."

While the first wave of DFSS Projects often has startling benefits, the real power of Design for Six Sigma is realized as you mature the integration of DFSS into your new product and service introduction process, which might be called the new DFSS product and service introduction process.

Companies that effectively accomplish this level of maturation in DFSS will command almost insurmountable competitive advantages. The tsunami of DFSS is coming. Ride the leading edge to win the new global competitive race that has already begun.

GLOSSARY

Critical to Quality (CTQ) A measurement that determines the elements of a process or product that are most critical to quality in the eyes of the customer.

Failure Mode and Effects Analysis (FMEA) A tool to help predict how things can fail, what the effect of the failure will be, how often the failure will occur, how severe the failure will be, how well the failure can be detected, and what controls can be implemented to reduce the probability of failure.

Ideal Function The desired, customer-focused response if the design performed its intended function perfectly—in other words, with no variation; the perfect state of a system's intended function. For an engineered system, this is the state where there is no energy loss. Parameter Design for Robust Optimization is done based on the ideal function.

Kano Model A model that graphically represents the three types of customer needs: basic, performance, and excitement.

Modified Brainstorming Techniques (assumption busting, etc.) Tools to help generate new and different concepts. Assumption busting challenges existing constraints to encourage thinking of ways to eliminate the existing limitations.

Noise Factors Variables that affect the design's function and are either uncontrollable or too expensive to control or change. Examples are temperature at the product usage environment, aging, and manufacturing environment.

Parameter Design The process of finding the best combination of control factors, or design configurations, so that the design or process becomes insensitive to noise factors. It is also referred to as Robust Optimization. The most cost-effective approach to achieve a Robust Design.

Process Control The practice of monitoring a process's performance to determine when the performance drifts beyond a certain threshold, so countermeasures can be taken to re-establish the process integrity.

Project charter A summary of why the project is needed (in the business case section of the charter), how our customers will benefit (in the opportunity statement), how we will measure the success of the Project (in the goal statement), what the boundaries of the Project will be (scope), what activities will be required for the Project to succeed (Project plan), and who will be responsible for the completion of each activity (in the team members section). This is the blueprint detailing how the Project will unfold.

Pugh Concept Selection Technique A matrix that allows for subjective comparisons of multiple design concepts allowing new concepts to be created and evaluated so that, ultimately, the best concept is selected.

Quality Function Deployment (QFD) A systematic tool for translating customer requirements into appropriate company requirements at each stage of DFSS, from developing the concepts for the project through implementing manufacturing processes. In short, it enables the creation of customer-driven product development.

Quality Loss Function (QLF) A monetary approximation of the quality loss that occurs when a quality characteristic deviates from its target value; the cost, in dollars, of missing the mark.

Robust Design® The state where the product's performance is virtually minimally sensitive to factors causing variability (either in the manufacturing or user's environment) at the lowest cost. Robust Design is achieved by selecting a good concept, Parameter Design (Robust Optimization), and Tolerance Design. Robust Design is a registered trademark of the American Supplier Institute.

Robust technology An approach to optimize the robustness of technology elements so that they can be applied to family and future products. Optimization is done at technology level at the earliest stage, such as the research and development stage, contributing to minimize overall product development cycle time.

Taguchi Methods® Taguchi Methods is an engineering optimization strategy developed by Dr. Genichi Taguchi. It is a registered trademark of the American Supplier Institute.

Test to Failure This is a method for forcing failures to occur in the development cycle, so the weakest links can be identified early on and the appropriate corrections can be made before launching into production.

Tolerance Design The process of determining whether the cost to upgrade an individual component's tolerances, and to what degree, will result in an overall net reduction in loss. The process utilizes the Quality Loss Function to determine if the overall net loss reduction will justify the cost of upgrading components' tolerances.

TRIZ methodology A system for inventive problem solving developed by Genrich Altshuller; an approach to aid an individual to *systematically* innovate new concepts.

Voice of the Customer (VOC) The VOC describes the needs and desires customers seek from their products and service encounters, as expressed during interviews, surveys, and focus groups.

BIBLIOGRAPHY

Altshuller, Genrich. *The Innovation Algorithm: TRIZ, Systematic Innovation and Technical Creativity.* Worcester, Mass.: Technical Innovation Center, 1999.

———. *40 Principles: TRIZ Keys to Technical Innovation.* Worcester, Mass.: Technical Innovation Center, 1999.

Ashhenas, Ron, Dave Ulrich, Todd Jich, and Steve Hear. *The Boundaryless Organization: Breaking the Chains of Organizational Structure.* San Francisco: Jossey-Bass Publishers, 1995.

Breyfogle, Forrest W. *Implementing Six Sigma: Smarter Solutions Using Statistical Methods.* New York: Wiley, 1999.

Chowdhury, Subir. *The Talent Era: Achieving a High Return on Talent.* New York: Financial Times Prentice Hall, 2002.

———. *The Power of Six Sigma: An Inspiring Tale of How Six Sigma Is Transforming the Way We Work.* Chicago: Dearborn Trade, 2001.

———, ed. *Management 21C: Someday We'll All Manage This Way.* London: Financial Times Prentice Hall, 2000.

Crosby, Philip B. *Quality Is Free: The Art of Making Quality Certain.* New York: McGraw Hill, 1979.

Gale, Bradley T. *Managing Customer Value: Creating Quality and Service That Customers Can See.* New York: The Free Press, 1994.

Harry, Mikel, and Richard Schroeder. *Six Sigma: The Breakthrough Management Strategy Revolutionizing the World's Top Corporations.* New York: Doubleday, 2000.

Kaplan, Robert S., and David P. Norton. *The Balanced Scorecard.* Boston: Harvard Business School Press, 1996.

Kelley, Tom, with Jonathan Littman. *The Art of Innovation*. New York: Currency Doubleday, 2001.

Pande, Peter S., Robert P. Neuman, and Roland R. Cavanagh. *The Six Sigma Way: How GE, Motorola, and Other Top Companies Are Honing Their Performance*. New York: McGraw-Hill, 2000.

Porten, Michael E. *Competitive Advantage: Creating and Sustaining Superior Performance*. New York: The Free Press, 1985.

Revelle, Jack B., John W. Moran, and Charles A. Cox. *The QFD Handbook*. New York: John Wiley, 1998.

Senge, Peter M. *The Fifth Discipline: The Art and Practice of the Learning Organization*. New York: Doubleday, 1990.

Taguchi, Genichi, Subir Chowdhury, and Shin Taguchi. *Robust Engineering: Learn How to Boost Quality While Reducing Costs & Time to Market*. New York: McGraw-Hill, 1999.

Taguchi, Genichi, Subir Chowdhury, and Yuin Wu. *The Mahalanobis-Taguchi System*. New York: McGraw-Hill, 2000.

Terninko, John. *Step-By-Step QFD: Customer-Driven Product Design*. New York: St. Lucie Press, 1997.

Terninko, John, Alla Zusman, and Boris Zlotin. *Systematic Innovation: An Introduction to TRIZ (Theory of Inventive Problem Solving)*. New York: St. Lucie Press, 1998.

Tichy, Noel M., and Stratford Sherman. *Control Your Destiny or Someone Else Will: Lessons in Mastering Change—from the Principles Jack Welch Is Using to Revolutionize GE*. New York: HarperBusiness, 1993.

Welch, Jack, with John A. Byrne. *Jack: Straight from the Gut*. New York: Warner Books, 2001.

Wu, Yuin, and Alan Wu. *Taguchi Methods for Robust Design*. New York: ASME Press, 2000.

ACKNOWLEDGMENTS

I would like to extend enormous gratitude to the man who taught all of us the power of Robust Engineering—Dr. Genichi Taguchi. I am very fortunate to work very closely with this genius. His teaching inspires me every day.

Dr. Armand V. Feigenbaum, Philip B. Crosby, and J. D. Power III have also been a great inspiration to me. Their continuous support of my work is extremely valuable. I honor and respect all of them.

A great talent who helped me to refine the manuscript with integrity and a sense of quality is my friend John Bacon. I feel a deep sense of gratitude to John for his enormous support and hard work, and for helping me.

My two dear friends and colleagues in business, Shin Taguchi and Alan Wu, have been instrumental in making this book happen. They worked in the hotel room at 1:00 AM when required, to challenge my thoughts. Thank you both for your continuous support.

My colleague and friend, Dr. Barry Bebb, is a phenomenal researcher. Barry, thank you for your hard work on the manuscript and continuous challenge.

My colleague Brad Walker helped me on the book during the holiday seasons. A young consultant, Brad is always striving for the best. Thank you, Brad.

Thanks to my colleagues Jim Wilkins, John Terninko, Dave Kesselring, and Bill Eureka for their continuous hard work on Six Sigma and DFSS deployment at different organizations.

Thanks to my Dearborn Trade editor, Jean Iversen, for her project leadership and continuous challenge.

Thanks also to my very special friend in the publishing business, Cynthia Zigmund, publisher at Dearborn Trade, for her belief in every one of my writing ventures from the first day I met her, and for her continuous encouragement.

I extend my gratitude to everyone at Dearborn Trade for their hard work: Sandy Thomas, Leslie Banks, Robin Bermel, Mindi Rowland, Paul Mallon, and Jack Kiburz.

Thanks to all of my dear friends and colleagues in the business, especially everyone at ASI—American Supplier Institute—for their assistance and help.

All my friends in the Six Sigma business, including AIT Group, BMG, and George Group, have given me continuous support. Thank you.

I am also grateful to my parents, Sushil and Krishna Chowdhury, and to my in-laws, Ashim and Krishna Guha, for their constant demonstration of love.

This book would never have become a reality without the support of my lovely wife Malini. Of course, the real joy in my daily life comes from my little daughter Anandi.

INDEX

ABOUT THE AUTHOR

Subir Chowdhury is executive vice president at ASI–American Supplier Institute—the world's premier consulting and training firm on Design for Six Sigma and Robust Engineering. Prior to ASI, he served as a quality management consultant at General Motors Corporation. Hailed by the *New York Times* as a "leading quality expert," Chowdhury was also recognized by *Quality Progress* of the American Society for Quality as one of the "Voices of Quality in the 21st Century."

Author of seven books, Chowdhury's most recent international bestselling books include *The Power of Six Sigma* and *Management 21C: Someday We'll All Manage This Way.* His books have been translated into more than ten languages. He is frequently cited in the national and international media.

Chowdhury has received numerous international awards for his leadership in quality management and major contributions to the automotive industry. Chowdhury was honored by the Automotive Hall of Fame, and the Society of Automotive Engineers awarded him its most prestigious recognition, the Henry Ford II Distinguished Award for Excellence in automotive engineering. He also received the honorable U.S. Congressional Recognition. From 1999 to 2000, he served as chairman of the American Society for Quality's Automotive Division. In 2002, the Society of Manufacturing Engineers honored Chowdhury with its most prestigious international honor, "SME Gold Medal."

Chowdhury lives with his wife, Malini, and daughter, Anandi, in Novi, Michigan.

HOW TO CONTACT ASI

If you enjoyed reading this book and require assistance on Design for Six Sigma and/or Six Sigma implementation processes, contact:

ASI–American Supplier Institute
38705 Seven Mile Road, Suite 345
Livonia, MI 48152
Phone: 800-462-4500 or 734-464-1395
Fax: 734-464-1399
Web site: <www.asiusa.com>

For specific inquiries, contact:

Dave Waggoner
ASI Vice President of Business Development
Phone: 800-462-4500, extension 213
E-mail: dave.waggoner@asiusa.com

THE *ONLY* WAY TO ACHIEVE
SIX SIGMA IS WITH DFSS

ORDER IN QUANTITY to communicate this message with all of your Six Sigma leaders. Contact Mindi Rowland in Special Sales at 800-621-9621, extension 4410, or by e-mail at rowland@dearborn.com.

Your company also can order this book with a customized cover featuring your name, logo, and message.

Dearborn™
Trade Publishing
A **Kaplan Professional** Company